DEALING WITH DOMESTIC VIOLENCE AND CHILD ABUSE

Society's Judicial Disgrace!

ROBERTA CAVA

Copyright © 2015 by Roberta Cava

This book is licensed for your personal enjoyment only and may not be re-sold or given away to other people. If you would like to share this book with another person, please purchase an additional copy for each recipient. If you're reading this book and did not purchase it or it was not purchased for your use only, then please purchase your own copy. Thank you for respecting the hard work of this author.

Dealing with Domestic Violence and Child Abuse
- *Society's Judicial Disgrace!*
Roberta Cava

Published by Cava Consulting
info@dealingwithdifficultpeople.info

Discover other titles by Roberta Cava at
www.dealingwithdifficultpeople.info

National Library of Australia

Cataloguing-in-publication data:

Originally published in eBook format in 2005

ISBN 978-0-9923402-2-3

BOOKS BY ROBERTA CAVA

Non-Fiction

Dealing with Difficult People
(23 publishers – in 17 languages)
Dealing with Difficult Situations – at Work and at Home
Dealing with Difficult Spouses and Children
Dealing with Difficult Relatives and In-Laws
Dealing with Domestic Violence and Child Abuse
Dealing with School Bullying
Dealing with Workplace Bullying
Retirement Village Bullies
Keeping Our Children Safe
What am I going to do with the rest of my life?
Before tying the knot – Questions couples Must ask each other Before they marry!
How Women can advance in business
Survival Skills for Supervisors and Managers
Human Resources at its Best!
Human Resources Policies and Procedures - Australia
Employee Handbook
Easy Come – Hard to go – The Art of Hiring, Disciplining and Firing Employees
Time and Stress – Today's silent killers
Take Command of your Future – Make things Happen
Belly Laughs for All! – Volumes 1 to 4
Wisdom of the World! The happy, sad and wise things in life!

Fiction

That Something Special
Something Missing
Trilogy: Life Gets Complicated
Life Goes On
Life Gets Better

ACKNOWLEDGEMENTS

Special thanks to Tim Field (of website "Bully OnLine" in the UK) for his valuable contributions that are used throughout this book. Many thanks to the victims of domestic violence and child abuse who took the time to tell me their horror stories.

Many thanks to Dr. Joseph Carver, Ph. D. Clinical Psychologist, Ohio (see Chapter 3); Doreen Orion, MD, "I Know You Really Love Me;" David Kinchin, "Post Traumatic Stress Disorder: The Invisible Injury;" Frances Cearns, Lenore Walker, Karen Neilsen and Edmonton Area Inter-Agency Committee on Wife Assault Sources, "Wife Assault - Hurts All of Us;" Domestic Violence Service, Gold Coast, Queensland, "Domestic Violence - an Information Book;" Dr. Stanton E. Samenow, "Straight Talk about Criminals" and "Inside the Criminal Mind;" Expatica "Parents Banned from Smacking Children;" Australian Institute of Health and Welfare, "A Picture of Australia's Children;" Robert Glade-Wright, "Living with the cost of abuse;" Office of Women's Policy, Department for Victorian Community, "Growing Victoria Together" and "Women's Safety Strategy;" Mission Australia, "Project Circuit Breaker;" Barnardos, "Neglect hurts more when you do nothing about it;" and Elaine Hollingsworth, "Smoke Gets in your Eyes" for giving me permission to use their information.

Memorial to Tim Field:

Tim Field died on January 15, 2006 at the age of 53 from cancer. He was a world authority on bullying and psychiatric injury and author of the best-selling Bully in Sight (1997). His vision was to attain a bully-free world and he campaigned in schools, further and higher education and the workplace to achieve this.

He lectured all over the world and worked personally on more than 5,000 bullying cases, highlighting the lack of understanding for victims. He revealed patterns showing how trade unions often failed to deal effectively with the problem among their members.

Field believed that bullying was the single most important social issue today. His work inspired and influenced international anti-bullying organisations, while his personal energy, commitment and knowledge restored sanity and saved lives. The world misses this dedicated anti-bullying campaigner.

Dealing with Domestic Violence &Child Abuse
Society's Judicial Disgrace!

Table of contents

Introduction	*1*
Chapter 1; What is bullying?	*3*

- Kinds of abuse;
- What is bullying?
- Kinds of bullies;
- Physical;
- Verbal;
- Pornography;
- Female;
- Group;
- Bullies who were victims;
- Road rage;
- Stalkers;
- Who are the targets?
- Where are people bullied?
- How do you know the person is a bully?
- Workplace serial bullies.

Chapter 2; Health disorders related to domestic violence   15

- Antisocial Personality Disorder (APD);
- Psychopath;
- Narcissistic Personality Disorder;
- Sociopath;
- Psychosis vs neurosis;
- The gender differences;
- What are the results to the victim/targets of bullying?
- What is Post Traumatic Stress Disorder (PTSD)?
- Depression;
- Stress breakdown;
- Self-harm.

Chapter 3; Help from Dr. Joseph Carver, Ph.D.   25

- Emotional memory management: positive control over your memory;
- Daily memory;
- How files affect us;
- Rules;
- Serotonin;
- Dopamine;
- Nor epinephrine;
- Endorphins;
- Files and depression;
- Files and physical/mental trauma;
- Techniques for file control;
- Changing, destroying and contaminating old files;
- File control in special situations;
- Developing a treatment plan;
- The Loser – warning signs you're dating a loser (20 steps);
- Dangerous versions of the loser;
- Guidelines for detachment;
- Ending the relationship;
- Follow-up protection;
- Love and the Stockholm Symptom;
- The mystery of loving an abuser;
- Perceived threat to one's physical/psychological survival;
- The small kindness perception;
- Isolation from perspectives other than those of the captor;
- Perceived inability to escape.

Chapter 4; Spousal and partner abuse   63

- Domestic violence – an information book;
- Facts to ponder;
- Understanding domestic violence;
- Isolation;
- Spousal abuse;
- Drug and alcohol abuse;
- What about women who use violence?
- Mutual violence;

- Religion and domestic violence;
- Culture and Domestic violence;
- Abusers believe;
- Their victims believe;
- Safety;
- Dysfunctional homes;
- Factors relating to bullying and victimisation;
- Why do men abuse?
- Emotional or psychological abuse;
- Wife assault hurts all of us;
- Isolation or social abuse;
- Excessive jealousy;
- Intimidation;
- Physical abuse;
- Destruction of property or pets;
- Sexual abuse;
- Financial abuse;
- The effects of abuse on women;
- Self-esteem;
- Feeling of helplessness;
- Self-blame and guilt;
- Denying and minimising;
- Drug and alcohol abuse;
- Conforming to abusive behaviour;
- Counselling;
- Learning violent behaviour;
- Children who witness wife abuse;
- Infants;
- Pre-school and school-aged children;
- Adolescents;
- When parents separate or dad stops his violence;
- Cycle of abuse;
- Cycle of violence;
- Tension-building phase;
- Battering phase;
- Remorse and contrite phase;
- The abusive man;
- The need to control within intimate relationships;

- Taking responsibility;
- Denial and blaming;
- Dependency and lack of empathy;
- Change in the abusive man's behaviour;
- Transference of anger;
- Long battles;
- Explaining the behaviour of abused women.

Chapter 5; Case studies; Domestic Violence — 97

- Single Mom;
- Police Officer;
- Russ;
- Papua New Guinea;
- Diane;
- Stalking – Brisbane;
- Pornography;
- Garry;
- Domestic Violence Order;
- Women's Safety – Women's Voices;
- Judith.

Chapter 6; How to prevent and stop domestic violence — 113

- Stopping wife assault;
- Myths and realities of wife battering;
- Domestic Violence – an Information Book;
- Common questions and answers;
- How safe is your relationship?
- Safety planning;
- Avoid serious injury and escape violence;
- Leaving safely;
- Long-term safety after separation;
- Legal issues;
- What is a protection order?
- How will the protection order work?
- How to report a breach of order;
- What can witnesses do?
- Why do friends and family not help?
- Wife Assault – Hurts all of us;

- Laying assault charges;
- Building a support network;
- Shelters;
- Counselling;
- Legal Resources;
- Women's Safety Strategy;
- Implementation;
- Australian Assistance;
- Domestic violence regional offices;
- Elder abuse;
- Reporting abuse;
- How to help a battered woman;
- How couples can resolve battles without violence.

Chapter 7; Dealing with rape and stalkers   *141*

- Adult rape victims;
- How victims can be assisted;
- Date rape;
- Dating abuse;
- Dealing with stalkers.

Chapter 8; Child abuse   *149*

- What is child abuse?
- Sexual;
- Physical;
- Tactile;
- Existence;
- Religious or cult;
- Emotional neglect;
- Emotional abuse;
- Physiological;
- Neglect;
- Physical neglect;
- Smoke gets in your eyes;
- Royal Brisbane Hospital Research;
- Why does child abuse happen?
- How can you identify child abuse?
- Domestic violence and children;

- Reactions of children exposed to domestic violence;
- Reactions of adolescents exposed to domestic violence;
- Australian children at risk;
- A picture of Australian children;
- Behavioural problems;
- Fathers renege from responsibilities;
- Paedophiles;
- Paedophiles in the workplace;
- How to protect children from sexual abuse;
- For Children;
- For Parents;
- If your child becomes a victim of sexual abuse.

Chapter 9; Case studies; Child abuse   171

- 18-month old twins starved to death;
- Child sex abuse cases;
- Abusive parents hide behind legal loophole;
- Women's Safety ; Women's Voices;
- Julie;
- Monster Dad;
- Janet;
- Debra.

Chapter 10; How to prevent and stop child Abuse   177

- Reporting child abuse;
- What happens after a report of child sexual abuse
- How to help an abused child;
- Living with the cost of abuse;
- Project Circuit Breaker;
- Bernardos;
- Queensland Government;
- Parents banned from smacking children;
- How to deal with child bullies;
- What are the results to the bully?
- Differences between child and adult bullies;
- Dealing with child bullies;
- Dealing with the victims.

Chapter 11; Good Parenting   *191*

- Super Nanny;
- Battling children;
- Tantrums;
- The "Terrible Two's;"
- Street-proofing your child;
- Street-smart kids;
- How can you help?
- What to do if you need to leave your children at home alone;
- Out of control teens;
- Tough love;
- Disciplining when angry;
- To spank or not to spank?
- Skill of feedback;
- After discipline;
- Preparing your child for society;
- What children need from their parents.

Conclusion   *207*

Bibliography   *211*

Web Connections   *215*

INTRODUCTION

Abuse of any kind is abhorrent to everyone except the bullies that use it. Bullying behaviour, more often than not, starts in the home. There's a lot of anecdotal evidence to suggest that people who are bullies as adults were bullies at home and at school and learned they could get away with it.

Children watch how their parents and siblings settle disputes. Children copy what they see - and if they see their role models settling disputes with violence, they will copy that behaviour. They will likely bully siblings, friends and those in day-care facilities. If conflicts are settled by negotiation and discussion, children learn to use their heads instead of their fists or bullying behaviour to deal with difficult situations. However, if the parents (their role models) deal with disputes by having shouting matches or using aggressive behaviour - their children are likely to clone this behaviour.

If this unacceptable behaviour is not stopped - it will naturally go with the child into our schools. Do all children from such homes become bullies - of course not, but the apple seldom falls far from the tree. Under most circumstances, the bullying child will have bullying parents.

And then there's the school system. Slowly, but surely government bodies have taken the control away from teachers and administrators. These teachers are forced to teach at the level of the lowest common denominator in their classes and spend much of their valuable time trying to re-channel the energies of their hyperactive or bullying students. There are too many students per teacher, so teachers spend less time with each child. School curriculum puts heavy emphasis on knowledge and little on how to work co-operatively with others. And, sometimes teachers and schools find it easier to "look the other way" when faced with bullying episodes.

This book stresses that if we don't start at the beginning (in the home) the problem will not change. Unless we stop bullying in our schools and give teachers more authority to deal with those bullies - the message will remain that bullying behaviour (although not condoned) is allowed. If bullies get away with their actions at home and at school - their next targets are in the workplace.

Every day, women are sexually assaulted, date-raped and beaten or killed by their husbands and partners. For some reason we have accepted this. But if we don't stop it by enforcing laws that stop these actions, they will simply continue. How can you help? If you care about yourself, your mother, your sister or your neighbour and see that they are being abused, help stop the violence by giving assistance to the battered woman or ask for it yourself. Fight persistently that stronger laws be put into place and enforced with the full might of the law.

The cycle of abuse must end. Only by keeping the public aware of the travesties being committed against wives and children, will a solution be found. I live in Australia's and its macho image needs serious revision. The beating of wives and/or children is not masculine - it's cowardice.

Those bullying cowards know of no other way to live life except to overpower others. To deal with the serious problems these bullies cause, we must demand that our politicians and courts toughen up our legal system so that society (and the laws) have zero-tolerance to any violent act. Until legal zero-tolerance laws are enforced, the peaceful citizens will not be properly protected from the bullying behaviour that seems to permeate the world.

Chapter 1
WHAT IS BULLYING?

Although this book is about school bullying, it's important to know the different kinds of abuse, because bullies are often abusive in many areas of their lives.

Bullying is a pattern of constant, daily fault-finding, criticism, segregation, exclusion and undermining that occurs for weeks or months. Each incident can be trivial and on their own do not represent an offence or grounds for disciplinary action. The average bullying episode is brief, approximately 37 seconds long, but emotional scars from bullying can last a lifetime. Recovery from a bullying experience can take between two to five years and some people never fully recover. Bullying differs from harassment and assault because the latter can result from a single incident or a small number of incidents, whereas bullying tends to be an accumulation of many small incidents over a long period of time.

The most despicable bullies on this earth are terrorists, murderers, rapists, paedophiles and pimps. These dregs of the earth all have one insatiable and obsessive need - to control others. They know of no other way to live life except to overpower others. However, they're cowards and have yellow streaks down their backbones. Anyone who feels confident about him- or herself does not need to use power to influence or control others.

This control is gained through terror, intimidation, harassment or just plain aggressiveness. The extrovert bullies tend to be shouters and screamers - are highly visible and bully from the top. A discussion becomes a debate and often ends up in a shouting match. They manipulate others into believing that they caused the bullying behaviour. Introverted bullies (the most dangerous types) tend to sit in the background and recruit others to do the bullying for them.

Bullies are cunning, conniving, scheming, calculating, sadistic, violent, cruel, nasty, ruthless, treacherous, pre-meditated, exploitive, parasitic, obnoxious, opportunist, ominous, menacing, sinister, ferocious, forceful, annoying and aggressive. They are experts in the use of sarcasm but lack communication, interpersonal and social skills. Some rely excessively or exclusively on emails or third parties and other strategies for avoiding face-to-face contact.

Rational human beings strive to coexist with others. Bullies don't understand this concept. Their need to control can reach obsessive heights and they can even have panic attacks if they feel they're not in control of every situation. These are sick people.

Bullies like pimps, relish having control over other human beings. However, they are insecure cowards whose only source of confidence is to be in control of situations and of others. This control is gained through terror, intimidation, harassment or just plain aggressiveness.

Bullies lack emotional intelligence. Emotional intelligence helps people understand and control their own emotions. It also helps them recognise and respond correctly to others' emotions. Those with emotional intelligence recognise emotions in others and know how to control their reactions to those emotions. They also know their own emotions and how to control them when they are getting upset or angry. Bullies are either born without emotional intelligence or they suppress it by copying their defective role models. Often extensive counselling is the only way to change their destructive behaviour.

Abuse is defined in the dictionary as "an evil or corrupt practice; deceit, betrayal, molestation, violation" and comes in many forms. The common denominator of all abuse is the collection of behaviours related to bullying.

- Abusers *choose* to abuse,
- Molesters *choose* to molest,
- Rapists *choose* to rape,
- Harassers *choose* to harass,
- Paedophiles *choose* to abuse children and
- Bullies *choose* to bully.

Symptoms of bullying

- Being belittled, demeaned or patronised especially in front of others. This chips away at the person's status, self-confidence, worth and potential;
- Being disgraced, shouted at and threatened, often in front of others;
- Making snide comments to see if the person will fight back;

- Treating them differently by showing favouritism to others and bias towards the victim;
- An unvarying refusal to recognise the victim's contributions;
- Finding fault and criticising everything the victim says and does or twisting, distorting and misrepresenting the victim. The criticism is of a trivial nature and often contains a grain of truth. This can dupe the victim into believing the criticism is valid.

Forms of bullying

- Terrorism and murder;
- Child abuse; child sexual abuse and child neglect;
- Pimping (selling of prostitution);
- Wife battering (domestic violence);
- School bullies;
- Armed forces bullying;
- Elderly abuse;
- Sports sexual abuse;
- Prison bullying;
- Road and queue rage;
- Stalking;
- Email abuse (on-line dating abuses);
- Neighbour abuse;
- Phone abuse;
- Cyber bullying;
- Workplace bullying;
- Sexual harassment: at work, at home, at school, in public (such as restaurants);
- Discrimination: age, sex, disabled, culture or nationality, religion;
- Mobbing (group bullying).

Where are people bullied?

- At home; (by parents, siblings or partners through bullying, assault, domestic violence, wife/child abuse, verbal abuse, neglect, emotional abuse);
- At school; (by other students, teachers or school staff);
- Under the care of others; (at child- or aged-care facilities – retirement villages – in hospitals, care homes, group homes, convalescent or rehabilitation facilities).

- At work; (by managers, clients, co-workers and subordinates through bullying/harassment, mobbing, falsifying time sheets, pilfering, embezzlement, fraud, malpractice, conspiracy, breaches of health and safety regulations, sexual harassment and/or discrimination);
- In prison; (by guards or other prisoners - by bullying, harassment, discrimination, assault);
- In the armed forces; (bullying, harassment, discrimination, assault);
- By those in authority; (harassment, abuse of power);
- By neighbours, landlords and even friends; (bullying, stalking, harassment);
- By strangers in restaurants and in line-ups; (that can involve harassment, stalking, assault, sexual assault, rape, grievous bodily harm and even murder).
- On the road; (road rage).

Why do bullies bully?

Some bully because their role models (often their parents or older siblings) bully. It's natural for children to mimic the behaviour of these role models. Others seem to be born with a lack of empathy towards others or a feeling that they are superior to others. It's almost impossible for these individuals to understand what their bullying behaviour does to their victims. Only professional counselling (lasting sometimes for years) can reverse these flawed individuals.

Who are the targets of bullying?

It is often assumed that victims of bullying are weak and inadequate. Targets of bullying are assumed to be loners, but most are independent, self-reliant and have no need for gangs or cliques. They have neither a need to impress nor are they interested in office politics. Bullies select individuals who prefer to use dialogue to resolve conflict and who will go to great lengths to avoid conflict. They constantly try to use negotiation rather than resorting to grievance and legal action. Targets are chosen because they are competent and popular. Bullies are jealous of the easy and stable relationships targets have with others.

Many targets are so traumatised by the bullying that they need professional help or take stress leave until the incidence of bullying is investigated. Bullies love this because they can claim that their target is "mentally ill" or "mentally unstable" or has a "mental health problem." It's much more likely that this allegation is a projection of the bully's own mental health problems which have not been treated.

Kinds of abuse

Bullying occurs in virtually all situations of life in which people interact with others. Thus we have bullying at home, at school, by caregivers in various situations, at work, in prison, in the armed forces, as neighbours interact and in public places through stalking, assault and road rage.

In terms of abuse and criminal acts in general, there are glaring differences between the genders. Young men are more likely to commit murder, arson, assault, fraud and sexual and drug-related offenses. For such acts, male offenders typically outnumber female offenders 4 to 1. As many of the factors causing bullying and abuse also lead to these behaviours, we need to give proper guidance to our boys and young men.

Although this book is about domestic violence and child abuse, it is important to know the different kinds of abuse, because bullies are often abusive in many areas of their lives. There are many kinds of abuse:

Violence: this includes wife and child battering, violent crime such as murder and road rage. Intimidation and threats on the telephone or from neighbours are also a form of violence.

Bullying: This form of abuse occurs in schools, in prison, in the military and at the workplace. Elderly people and children may also be bullied on account of their age.

Sexual abuse: Sexual harassment occurs at work, home, school and in places such as restaurants. This form of abuse also includes child sexual harassment, rape in all its forms and online dating abuse.

Discrimination: This is done on grounds of age, sex, disability, culture, nationality and religion.

Other forms of abuse: These include child neglect, stalking, pornography, road rage, queue rage and arson.

Kinds of bullies

- Adult bullies in the workplace;
- Abusive and violent partners;

- Abusive and violent parents;
- Abusive and violent children (abuse their parents and others);
- Abusers of those in care;
- Bullying neighbours, landlords, authorities;
- Con artists and swindlers;
- Cult leaders;
- Child bullies who can grow up to be adult bullies;
- Racial and sexual harassers;
- Sexual abusers and paedophiles;
- Rapists (also date rape) and those who commit acts of sexual violence;
- Advocates of hard pornography;
- Stalkers;
- Arsonists;
- Violent offenders including organised serial killers.

They are also found in a variety of situations:

Physical Bullies:

They act out their anger in physical ways. They resort to hitting or kicking their victims or damaging the victim's property. Of all the types of bullies, this one is easiest to identify because his or her behaviour is so obvious. This is the type of bully our imagination conjures up when we picture a bully. As they get older, physical bullies can become more aggressive in their attacks. As adults this aggressive attitude is so deeply ingrained in the bully's personality that serious long-term counselling is required to change the behaviour.

Verbal Bullies:

It is quite difficult for a victim to ignore this type of bully. They use words to hurt and humiliate, resorting to name-calling, insulting, teasing and making racist, chauvinistic or paternalistic comments. While this type of bullying does not result in physical scars, its effects can be devastating. It is often the easiest form of attack for a bully. It is quick and painless for the bully, but often remarkably harmful for the victim.

Pornography:

Pornography has been a traditional outlet for sexual frustration and probably always will be. Its acceptability is determined by current social values. Most people do not object to "soft" pornography and may even secretly indulge occasionally in order to see what they are missing. The harder the pornographic content, the more abusive it tends to be. The individual's need and hence dependency on pornography is directly proportional to that individual's feelings of sexual inadequacy.

Female Bullies:

Society makes the assumption that in a violent situation, there is a male aggressor and a female victim but females can be as vicious as males. Female bullies are spiteful, devious, manipulative and vengeful. These individuals use gossip and backstabbing to undermine, discredit or devaluate other's contributions. They have poorly-defined moral and ethical boundaries and put others down to make themselves feel important. They are experts in the use of sarcasm but lack communication, interpersonal and social skills.

Group Bullies:

These are predominantly female bullies who exclude their victims from feeling part of a group. They exploit the feeling of insecurity in their victims, by ambushing their victims and convincing peers to exclude or reject the victim. They often use the same tricks that the verbal bullies use with their victims to isolate them. Spreading nasty rumours about the victim is part of the pattern. It can be an extremely harmful form of bullying especially in children when they are making their first social connections, because it excludes the victim from his or her peer group.

Bullies who were victims:

Some bullies have been bullied or abused themselves. There is evidence that many murderers, especially those involving serial killings, have received brain damage from parental beatings. Those beatings can leave them with the inability to control their violent tendencies.

The first time bullies get a taste of their own medicine, they run whining to authorities for protection. They bully to feel competent, to get some relief from their own feelings of powerlessness. They are stuck between the state of a victim and a bully and are usually the most difficult to identify because they, at first glance, appear to be targets of other bullies and fiercely attack their bullies. They are usually impulsive and react quickly to intentional or unintentional physical encounters, claiming self-defence for their actions. Rather than lashing out at his or her bully, this victim needs to learn how to avoid other bullies.

Many abusers, molesters, harassers and bullies who end up in court because of their actions insist they were victims too.

These bullies seem to rely on their past problems as a victim to gain supporters. Such "do-gooders" will take advantage of any form of support they can get to evade taking responsibility for their actions. When asked to account for the way they choose to behave, bullies use a variety of strategies to evade accountability such as denial, counter-attack and feigned victimhood.

They are experts at buck-passing. They have not learned how to take responsibility for their actions, lack self-discipline and will often blame someone else for why they reacted as they did.

Road Rage:

Bullies are also prone to road rage. Road rage occurs when one driver expresses his or her anger towards another driver for something s/he did on the road. People are encouraged to engage in road rage by the fact that they will not see each other again. They also feel that the other motorist is just some idiot who has endangered their lives. Road rage can be expressed through screaming, beeping the horn, flashing headlights, slamming on the brakes to teach a tailgater a lesson, cutting a person off to retaliate, throwing things, hostile stares, sticking out the middle finger and profanities. Others even get out of their cars and start fighting.

Most people who demonstrate road rage are aggressive drivers, but do not consider their actions a problem to others. They think of the other drivers as being stupid, rude and discourteous. The stresses of modern urban life are no reason to take it out on other drivers.

Stalkers:

Stalkers include intimate partner stalkers, delusional stalkers and vengeful stalkers. Studies show that the overwhelming number of stalkers is men and the overwhelming number of their victims is women.

Intimate partner stalkers refuse to believe that the relationship has ended. The vast majority of these stalkers are not lonely people who are still hopelessly in love. On the contrary, they are emotionally abusive and controlling both during and after the relationship has ended. The only thing to say to the stalker is *"No"* once only and then never say anything to him again. If the stalker cannot have his victim's love, he will settle for her hatred or her fear. The worst thing in the world for stalkers is to be ignored.

Delusional stalkers frequently have had little, if any, contact with their victims. They may have major illnesses like schizophrenia, manic-depression or erotomania. In erotomania, the stalker's delusional belief is that the victim loves him and he believes that he is having a relationship even though they might never have met. Another more tenacious type might believe that he is destined to be with someone and that if he only pursues her hard enough and long enough, she will come to love him. Most are unmarried and socially immature.

The vengeful stalker is driven by vengeance, rather than love. They become angry with their victims over some slight, either real or imagined. This could be anger at a politician because of some piece of legislation they introduced or it could be disgruntled ex-employees.

Queue Rage

Public servants are being bashed, stalked and threatened with weapons in unprecedented abuse from customers forced to wait in long queues and being forced to fill in official forms. In one case they found the name of the person on the other side of the counter, found out where she lived and followed her. This employee's health has been totally destroyed and she will never be able to work again. Others have been threatened with syringes. Government employees at all levels are vulnerable to the danger. This could be classed as workplace abuse and their employers need to know this. By not having enough employees available to "service" their clients, they are setting their staff up for abuse by the clients.

The alarming increase in queue rage has prompted special training programs for frightened counter staff. This behaviour includes people jumping the counter, threatening, jumping the queue and performing in the waiting area for the benefit of others. And the public servants are wilting. Society in general and clients being served by government staff are more aware of their rights now than ever before. This has made them become more assertive and they can become very angry when trying to get what they want.

Employees are being trained to recognise the danger signals. They see clients fuming and know something is happening. This is where an alert supervisor can anticipate trouble. Employees are given alarm bells and a system of security that they can use if the situation escalates into abusive behaviour.

Cyber Bullying

Cyber bullying occurs when an adult or child is tormented, threatened, harassed, humiliated, embarrassed or otherwise targeted by another adult or child, using the Internet, interactive and digital technologies or mobile phones.

Cyber bullying is usually not a one-time communication, unless it involves a death threat or a credible threat of serious bodily harm. In extreme cases people have killed each other or committed suicide after being involved in a cyber bullying incident.

Adults too are being cyber bullied by their exes. Abusive spouses hack cars and household appliances to stalk, spook and spy on exes with high-tech cyber harassment. They change security alarms, control lights, air conditioners and monitor the movements of former partners. Surveillance devices have been placed in teddy bears, in the lining of a purse and even under floorboards. Victims are being urged to have their homes and belongings checked for devices.

Penalties for Cyber Bullying

Most of the time the cyber bullying does not go so far that the law intervenes, although victims often might attempt to lodge criminal charges. Cyber bullying however, may result in a misdemeanour cyber harassment charge or if the bullying child is young enough may result in the charge of juvenile delinquency. It has to have a minor on both sides or at least have been instigated by a minor against another minor.

It typically can result in the person losing their ISP or IM accounts because they violated their terms of service rules. In some cases, if hacking or password and identity theft is involved, they can be charged with serious criminal charges by state and federal law enforcement agencies.

Cyber Bullying is NOT...

Once adults cyber bully children, it is called **cyber harassment or cyber stalking.**

Adult cyber-harassment or cyber stalking is not cyber bullying.

It isn't when adults are trying to lure children into offline meetings. That is called **sexual exploitation** or luring by a sexual predator. The methods used are limited only by the bully's imagination and access to technology. And the cyber bully one moment may become the victim the next. They often change roles, going from victim to bully and back again.

Preventing Cyber Bullying

Educating the kids about the consequences (losing their ISP or IM accounts) helps. Teaching them to respect others and to take a stand against bullying of all kinds helps too. Because their motives differ, the solutions and responses to each type of cyber bullying incident has to differ too. Schools can work with parents to stop and remedy cyber bullying. They can also educate the students on cyber-ethics and the law. If schools are creative, they can sometimes avoid the claim that their actions exceeded their legal authority for off-campus cyber-bullying actions.

Parents also need to understand that a child is just as likely to be a cyber bully as a victim of cyber bullying and often go back and forth between the two roles during one incident. They may not even realise that they are seen as a cyber bully.

How you can stop Cyber Bullying once it starts

There are two things parents must consider before anything else. Is your child at risk of physical harm or assault? And how are they handling the attacks emotionally?

If there is any indication that personal contact information has been posted online or any threats are made to your child, you must run, do not walk, to your local law enforcement agency. Take a print-out of all instances of cyber bullying to show them, but note that a print-out is not sufficient to prove a case of cyber-harassment or cyber bullying. You'll need electronic evidence and live data for that. It is crucial that all electronic evidence be preserved to allow the person to be traced and to take whatever action needs to be taken. The electronic evidence is at risk for being deleted by the Internet service providers unless you notify them immediately that you need those records preserved!

Parents need to be the ones students trust when things go wrong online and offline. Yet students often don't go to their parents. Why? It's because their parents have a tendency to over-react. Most children will avoid telling their parents about a cyber bullying incident fearing they will only make things worse.

Unfortunately they also sometimes under-react. They need to be supportive of their children and realise that these attacks can follow them into their otherwise safe home and wherever they go online. The risk of emotional pain is very real and very serious, so parents should not ignore their plight.

Sports Bullying

A recent report released in Italy on violence in sport by UNICEF, said nearly one in ten Australians had suffered sexual abuse in a sporting context. Sexual violence against children in sport in Australia could be as high as 8 per cent compared to Canada, where 2.6 per cent of children reported experiencing unwanted sexual touching.

Trisha Layhee, one of the report's authors said the rates of sexual violence may be much higher and work was needed to assess the issue. Dr. Layhee, who now heads the Hong Kong Sports Institute, said Australia was unique in the world for having a coaching culture that encouraged extreme psychological abuse.

'What we found was the complete normalisation of psychologically abusive behaviour by coaches, particularly at the elite level. I mean coaches screaming at kids,' she said.

Her survey of 370 elite and club athletes in Australia found 31 per cent of female and 21 per cent of male athletes reported sexual abuse under the age of 18. Of these, 41 per cent of females and 29 per cent of males said the abuse occurred in a sporting context.

Chapter 2
HEALTH DISORDERS ASSOCIATED WITH DOMESTIC VIOLENCE AND CHILD ABUSE

Diagnosis of abusers is challenging. How do you deal with a person who is a compulsive liar with a Jekyll and Hyde nature, is charming and glib, excels at deception and evasion of accountability?

Many abusers fit the criteria for ***Antisocial Personality Disorder (APD).*** Although most people think those with APD are associated with low socio-economic status and urban settings and tend to be of lower intelligence - this is not the case. They come from all environments.

These individuals have a complete disregard for and violate the rights of others and indicate at least three of the following symptoms:

- Fail to conform to social norms with respect to lawful behaviours by performing acts that are grounds for arrest;
- Deceitful by repeated lying, use of aliases and conning others for personal profit or pleasure;
- Impulsiveness - fail to see the consequences of their actions;
- Irritability and aggressiveness, indicated by repeated physical fights, assaults or verbal battles;
- Reckless disregard for the safety of self or others;
- Consistently irresponsible - repeated failure to sustain consistent work behaviour;
- Fail to honour their financial obligations;
- Lack remorse by being indifferent to or rationalising having hurt, mistreated or stolen from others;
- Belong to gangs and cliques that do not only appear in school-aged children, but at the highest executive level in business.

Many serial bullies would also meet many, if not all, of the clinical criteria for a ***Psychopath.*** Psychopaths lack remorse, guilt and conscience. Although many psychopaths meet the diagnostic criteria for antisocial personality disorder; not all do. Similarly, not all people with antisocial personality disorder meet the criteria for a psychopath. Not all psychopaths end up in prison. Industrial Psychopaths can thrive in business and many are found in management or executive positions.

The serial bully displays behaviour congruent with many of the diagnostic criteria for *Narcissistic Personality Disorder.* This is shown by a pervasive pattern of grandiosity and self-importance, the need for admiration and for the lack of empathy. People with this disorder overestimate their abilities and inflate their accomplishments, often appearing boastful and pretentious, have fantasies of unlimited success and/or power, while correspondingly underestimate and devalue the achievements and accomplishments of others.

They're contemptuous, envious and impatient with others and take advantage of others to achieve their own ends. They need power, prestige, drama and enjoy manipulating others. These qualities draw them top leadership positions, but at extreme levels of narcissism - the results can be disastrous.

Narcissists can become intolerant of criticism, unwilling to compromise and frequently surround themselves with sycophants (flatterers). While narcissists often appear to be ideal choices for leadership positions, they may fall victim to the distortions of their narcissistic tendencies that are reinforced by their position.

Some will fraudulently claim to have qualifications, experience, affiliations or associations that they don't have or are not entitled to. They have low self-esteem and need constant attention and admiration. They fish for compliments, expect superior service and for others to defer to them. They lack sensitivity and empathy especially when others don't react in the expected manner. They expect to receive before and above the needs of others and overwork those around them. They may form romantic or sexual relationships for the purpose of advancing their purpose or career, abuse special privileges and squander resources.

A *Sociopath* is an individual with many characteristics of APD and expresses his/her violence psychologically through constant criticism, sidelining, exclusion, undermining, etc. Sociopaths are usually highly intelligent, have higher socio-economic status and often come from middle-class families.

The term *"psychosis"* is applied to mental illness and the term *"neurosis"* to psychiatric injury. The main difference is that a psychotic person is unaware they have a mental problem whereas the neurotic person is aware - often acutely. The serial bully's lack of insight into his/her behaviour and its effect on others has the hallmarks of a psychosis, although this obliviousness would appear to be a choice, rather than a condition. They show these behaviours:

- Are very controlling of others. If someone resists, they are vicious in their attack to regain that control.
- They don't listen to others, lack conscience, show no remorse, are drawn to power, are emotionally cold and flat, dysfunctional, disruptive, divisive, rigid and inflexible, selfish, insincere, insecure, immature and lack interpersonal skills.
- They are vicious, criticising and vindictive in private - but charming in front of witnesses. (Others often don't see this side of their nature).
- Are very convincing or compulsive liars and when called upon, are able to fabricate authentic-sounding reasons for their behaviour.
- Are charming and convincing, which they use to make up for their lack of empathy.
- Hiding under their charming exterior is often sexual harassment, discrimination and racial prejudice.
- On the surface they seem very self-assured, but inside are very insecure people.
- They excel at deception - have vivid imaginations - are often very creative.
- They encourage feelings of shame, embarrassment, guilt and fear, for that is how all abusers - including child sex abusers – control and silence their victims.
- Show inappropriate attitudes to sexual matters or behaviour.
- Refuse to acknowledge value or praise others.
- When others describe their uncaring nature, they respond with impatience, irritability and aggression.
- Often have an overwhelming, unhealthy and narcissistic need to portray themselves as a wonderful, kind, caring and compassionate person, in contrast to their behaviour and treatment of others.
- Are oblivious to the discrepancy between how they like to be seen (and believe they are seen) and how they are actually seen.
- Are unaware of leadership qualities (maturity, decisiveness, assertiveness, trust and integrity) and bullying (immaturity, impulsiveness, aggression, distrust and deceitfulness).
- When called to account for their actions, they aggressively deny everything and then counter-attack with distorted or fabricated

criticism and allegations. If this is insufficient, they quickly feign being the victim, often bursting into tears (the purpose is to avoid answering the question and thus evade accountability by manipulating others through the use of guilt).

Some serial bullies show signs of passive/aggressive behaviour. These people can be very dangerous. They have a pathological reaction to authority and those they perceive are in positions of authority. They channel their aggression into passive behaviour by slowing down efforts of others and stonewall progress. They're very hard to detect and others often feel frustrated when dealing with them but don't always understand why.

As most of us grow up, we're faced with restrictions that are normal and necessary. People with this tendency have often been controlled excessively, so the person learns to control others without confrontation. They love the thrill of insubordination and it sometimes doesn't matter if they win, as long as it appears their opponents lose. They love to play win-lose games and put something over on others.

They use excuses such as: *'It's not my fault this didn't work, it's yours.'* They show frequent signs of helplessness - the simplest thing seems beyond their comprehension. They provoke a feeling of defensiveness when others are dealing with them. Most tasks are performed late or not at all. When prodded they become argumentative. They're backstabbers, gossipers and are often so good at it that others believe their falsehoods.

Most people display the above signs at one time or another. However, if this develops into being their normal behaviour, these people are likely passive-aggressive and others will have to remain on guard when dealing with them. Make sure they understand the consequences of their actions, *'If this happens again, I'll ...'* Confront them using facts when you 'catch them in the act.'

Some serious passive-aggressives have criminal tendencies. Although they insist that others adhere to the rules of society, they have an unwillingness to conform, believing these do not apply to them. These people get a thrill out of speeding, of drinking and driving - and getting away with it. In some, this tendency keeps accelerating because they require higher and higher levels of danger, thrills and excitement to keep them appeased.

The Gender Differences

The statistics for criminal actions are staggering and identify that we're not giving the proper guidance to our boys and young men:

- Young men have a 300 per cent higher death rate from motor vehicle accidents than young women;
- Jail inmates - 95 per cent male - 5 per cent female;
- Homicide - 85 per cent male - 15 per cent female;
- Arson - 86 per cent male - 14 per cent female;
- Assault - 82 per cent male - 18 per cent female;
- Sexual offences - 98 per cent male - 2 per cent female;
- Manslaughter by driving - 80 per cent male – 20 per cent female;
- Malicious damage to property - 87 per cent male – 13 per cent female;
- Blackmail - 92 per cent male - 8 per cent female;
- Drug offences - 82 per cent male - 18 per cent female;
- Fraud - 63 per cent male - 37 per cent female;
- Shoplifting - 60 per cent male - 40 per cent female.

What are the results to the victim/target of bullying?

- The victims' constant high stress level interferes with their immune system causing frequent illnesses such as the flu, ulcers, irritable bowel problems, skin problems such as eczema, psoriasis, athlete's foot, shingles, colds, coughs, ear, nose and throat infections.
- Their body's batteries never have an opportunity to recharge.
- They suffer from aches and pains in the joints and muscles or have back pain with no obvious cause that won't go away or respond to treatment.
- They're disempowered such that they become dependent on the bully to allow them to get through each day without their life being made hell.
- Initially they're reluctant to take action against their bullies and report them knowing that they could accelerate the abuse. Later this gives way to a strong urge to take action against the bullies so that others don't have to suffer a similar fate.

The targets have:

- An overwhelming desire for acknowledgement, understanding, recognition and validation of their experience and strong motivation for justice to be done;
- An unwillingness to talk or interact with the bully;
- An unusually strong sense of vulnerability, victimisation or persecution;
- An unusually strong desire to educate the public and help the public introduce domestic violence and child abuse prevention laws;
- An overwhelming sense of betrayal and an inability or unwillingness to trust anyone;
- Headaches and migraines;
- Shattered self-confidence and low self-esteem;
- Become seriously depressed, especially upon waking;
- Become tired, exhausted and lethargic;
- Found their levels of guilt are abnormally high which may preclude them from starting new relationships;
- Found themselves constantly fatigued (similar to Chronic Fatigue Syndrome) or sweat, tremble, shake or have heart palpitations;
- Suffered from panic attacks triggered by any reminder of the experience;
- Physical numbness (toes, fingertips, lips) and emotional numbness (especially the inability to feel joy);
- Impaired memory that's due to suppressing horrific memories;
- Found they're constantly on edge mentally – have a short fuse and are irritated, especially by small insignificant events;
- Often been highly upset by the amount of anger they feel towards their abuser and are horrified by the mental pictures of creative, cruel, torturous ways they could pay back their abuser;
- Constantly been on alert because their fight or flight mechanism has become permanently activated;
- Become hypersensitive and inappropriately perceive almost any remark as critical;
- Found that work becomes difficult, often impossible to undertake;
- Become obsessed with the abusive experience that takes over their lives, eclipsing and excluding almost every other interest;
- Believed that their abusive problems are hopeless and that their efforts to stop it will be futile;

- Been sleepless, have nightmares, constantly relive events, wake early or wake up more tired than when they went to bed;
- Poor concentration and become forgetful especially with trivial day-to-day things;
- Experienced regular intrusive, violent visualisations and flashbacks and can't get the abuse out of their minds;
- Become emotional - bursting into tears regularly over trivial matters;
- Become uncharacteristically irritable, have angry outbursts, are hypersensitive and feel fragile;
- Feelings of withdrawal and isolation, want to be on their own and seek solitude;
- Suffered from post-traumatic stress disorder (PTSD).

Post traumatic stress following victimisation is largely due to the shattering of basic assumptions victims hold about themselves and the world. Specifically that:

- The world is kind, caring, compassionate, generous, giving;
- The world is meaningful;
- I am worthy.

For the targets that become victims of abuse, their world and self-view is shattered and they may find it impossible to function normally or effectively. Research would indicate that often those who suffer most from unacceptable abusive behaviour are those with the most to give - those with high expectations of themselves and those who are prepared to go the extra mile because they believe that what they do is meaningful and important.

What is Post Traumatic Stress Disorder (PTSD)?

David Kinchin estimates in his book ***Post Traumatic Stress Disorder: the invisible injury*** www.bullyonline.org/stress/davidk.htm that at any time, around one per cent of the population is experiencing PTSD. Within some groups of society, the incidence of PTSD must be expected to be much higher than one per cent.

Post Traumatic Stress Disorder PTSD is a natural emotional reaction to a deeply shocking and disturbing experience. There is growing recognition that PTSD can result from many types of shocking experiences including an accumulation of small, individually non-life-threatening events. These situations are called Complex PTSD. The individual experiencing trauma feels s/he is unable to escape the situation. Traumatic situations of domestic, school and workplace abuse can be extremely difficult to get out of.

Sometimes those who are abused thinks they are going mad. They are not; PTSD is an injury, not an illness. The silent suffering could be considerable, but those who suffer - mostly unnecessarily - are prevented from realising their potential and contributing fully to society and to industry. Many sufferers of Complex PTSD are hard workers who are reluctant to claim health benefits.

Depression

Stress or more appropriately *'distress'* occurs when an individual believes that the demands or perceived demands of a situation outweigh his/her ability or perceived ability to cope with the situation. The coping mechanisms under challenge include those the person needs to resolve the problem, be it emotional, familial, work-related or otherwise. From a psychological viewpoint, depression occurs when the individual feels his/her world is consistently unpleasant, punishing or deprives them of the opportunity for a positive and satisfying life. Their negative experiences may be compounded by feelings of being unable to change their situation - a process of learned helplessness.

Individuals with depression expect and predict that their unpleasant and distressing experiences will continue into the future. Guilt-ridden perceptions of being responsible for their own distress, either through the things they have done or not done or negative thoughts about their inability to cope, add to the depressed feelings. The combination of a negative view of their lives, the expectation that it will continue, the self-criticism or self-blame for the situation, coupled with the inability to cope, are the characteristic psychological processes of depression.

Stress Breakdown

Stress breakdown differs from a nervous breakdown or mental breakdown that are the consequence of mental illness. Stress breakdown is a psychiatric injury, which is a normal reaction to an abnormal situation. The two types of breakdown are distinct and should not be confused. A stress breakdown is a natural and normal conclusion to a period of prolonged negative stress; the body is saying:

"I'm not designed to operate under these conditions of prolonged negative stress so I'm going to do something dramatic to ensure that you reduce or eliminate the stress. Otherwise, my body may suffer irreparable damage and I must take action now."

Dr. John T. O'Brien, consultant in old-age psychiatry at Newcastle General Hospital published a paper subtitled: ***Prolonged stress may cause permanent brain damage.***

A stress breakdown is often predictable, sometimes days or weeks in advance. The person's fear, fragility, obsessiveness, hyper-vigilance and hyper-sensitivity combine to evolve into paranoia. If this happens, a stress breakdown is only days or even hours away and the person needs urgent medical help. The risk of suicide at this point is heightened. Research says that young men are committing suicide at five times the rate as females.

Self-Harm

Self-harm is linked to abuse, unwanted pregnancy and parental divorce. One in 17 children is believed to hurt or self-harm itself. Behind these children is often a family in distress. Self-harm is the intentional cause to harm one's own body. These include: deliberate self-harm, self-injury, self-mutilation, self-abuse, self-wounding, self-inflicted violence, para-suicide, non-fatal act and wrist cutting. All these definitions of self-harm cover the same actions:

- Cutting;
- Burning skin by physical means using heat;
- Burning skin by chemical means using caustic liquids;
- Punching hard enough to cause bruises;
- Head banging;
- Hair pulling from head, eyelashes, eyebrows and armpits;
- Poisoning by ingesting small amounts of toxic substances to cause discomfort or damage;
- Insertion of foreign objects;
- Excessive nail biting to the point of bleeding and ripping cuticles;
- Excessive scratching by removing top layer of skin to cause a sore;
- Bone breaking;
- Gnawing at flesh;
- Wound interference to prevent wounds from healing thus prolonging the effect;

- Tying ligatures around the neck, arms or legs to restrict the flow of blood;
- Medication abuse without intention to die;
- Alcohol abuse;
- Illegal drug use;
- Smoking.

Cutting and burning are among the most common forms of self-harm. Those who are smoking and drinking are not consciously harming themselves; they are taking part in a socially accepted lifestyle. It is only once these actions become excessive that problems can occur.

There is also a strong correlation between eating disorders and self-harm. This is due to the fact that starvation, binge-eating and self-induced vomiting, overuse of laxatives and diuretics are forms of self-harm, as are starvation, binge-eating and vomiting.

Conclusion:

Bullying springs from deep-seated psychological problems that need to be identified. Victims of bullying also suffer many negative symptoms. The lives of these victims need to be carefully examined for these negative symptoms and they need to receive the appropriate help.

Chapter 3
HELP FROM DR. JOSEPH CARVER, PH.D.

Dr. Joseph Carver, Ph.D., Clinical Psychologist was kind enough to allow me to use excerpts from the following papers. To obtain the full articles, please go to his web page: www.drjoecarver.com

Emotional Memory Management: Positive Control Over Your Memory

Emotional Memory Management or EMM, is concerned with the thinking and memory part of brain functioning. Much like a modern-day computer, the brain stores memories in a system of files. In a manner that is still partially unknown, the brain has the ability to store not only memories but emotions as well - as they occurred at the time the memory was made.

Memory files thus contain two parts, the information about the event and the feeling we had at the time of the event. Studies tell us we can have two types of memory for the same situation, especially if the situation/experience is one associated with strong emotions. For a single experience (traumatic event, good event, emotional experience, etc.) we can have an explicit memory - a memory of the details of the experience and an implicit memory - a memory of the emotions connected to the experience.

Explicit memory has also been called "emotional memory" because it contains the memory of the physiological response at the time of the experience. This physiological response may include increased blood pressure, higher respiration, muscle tension, anxiety, fearfulness and other reactions associated with fear, terror, fright or even joy.

When we experience a very emotional event, the brain records not only the details of the experience (where we were, when, who was there, what happened, etc.) but the emotions we experienced at the time as well. The entire memory of an emotional event (an assault, an automobile accident, a wedding, death of a loved one, a combat experience, etc.) is actually remembered by two systems in the brain and stored in two separate areas of the brain.

If we remember the details of being assaulted, we will also experience the feelings we had at that time - the increased heart rate, fearfulness, panic and desperation. The brain also has the ability to remember one part of the memory without another part surfacing. This is the reality of Post-Traumatic Stress Disorder (PTSD) and emotional trauma. We may emotionally relive a combat memory when we hear a car backfire or emotionally feel as if we are being assaulted if someone jokingly grabs us from behind.

Daily Memory

A specific memory area of the brain will hold memories for about five days, to see if they are important. Memories that are not important are usually "dumped" or erased after the five-day waiting period. These erased memories can never be recovered. If a memory file containing only data is not frequently used, the memory slowly fades away. In short, if a daily memory does not have a strong good or bad emotional value, it is faded out.

As years pass, we build up quite a file system. We build up a collection of good memories and bad memories. Our brain has the ability to pull these memories at the drop of a hat - almost instantly. Importantly, you have no control over what file is pulled, how fast it is pulled or what is in the file. For example, younger adults and teenagers may have no "file" on the Kennedy assassination. They were not around at the time or old enough to make a memory of that experience.

Those with emotional memories can not only give you the exact details, but a variety of random and irrelevant details surrounding the event. This is how powerful "emotional memory" (EM) can be.

How Files Affect Us

Remember, the file contains two parts, information and emotion. Each rule will be explained in detail:

Rule: The brain operates on chemicals.

These chemicals produce emotional responses in the brain and body. Just like a certain combination of flour, sugar, butter and other foods can combine and produce a German chocolate cake, these chemicals combine in our brain to produce certain moods, reactions and feelings.

Just like an automobile contains various fluids (brake, window washer, transmission, oil, anti-freeze, etc.); the brain operates on chemicals known as "neurotransmitters." While the subject is too technical for this paper, it is known that these brain chemicals called "neurotransmitters" produce various emotional conditions. Like the oil in our automobile, neurotransmitters have a normal level in the brain and can be "low" or "high" depending upon certain situations. Some typical neurotransmitters:

Serotonin: Perhaps the most actively researched neurotransmitter at this time, serotonin is known to be related to depression, headaches, sleep problems and many mental health concerns. When serotonin is low in the brain system - depression and other mental health problems are produced. Low Serotonin is also associated with bulimia, a severe eating disorder, where the body craves sweets and carbohydrates in a desperate effort to raise serotonin levels. Antidepressants, such as Prozac and Zoloft, work by increasing serotonin in the brain. As our Serotonin level returns to normal, our depression lifts.

Dopamine: Abnormally high levels of this neurotransmitter in the brain produce paranoia, excitement, hallucinations and disordered thought (schizophrenia). Abnormally low levels produce motor or movement disorders such as Parkinson's Disease.

Nor epinephrine: Related to anxiety and depression, high levels in the brain produce strong physical-anxiety manifestations such as trembling, restlessness, smothering sensations, dry mouth, palpitations, dizziness, flushes, frequent urination and problems with concentration. A "panic attack" is actually a sudden surge of nor epinephrine in the brain.

Endorphins: Substances produced by the body that kill pain or produce a feeling of well-being. In marathon runners, these substances are responsible for the "runner's high." Also produced during pregnancy, a sudden increase near delivery-time creates that need to rearrange furniture, go dancing or clean house.

The levels of these chemicals or neurotransmitters in the brain create our mood. A chronic low level of serotonin, as when experiencing long-term severe stress, produces strong depression. The low serotonin creates symptoms such as:

- Frequent crying spells;
- Loss of concentration and attention;

- Early morning awakening (about 4:00 am);
- Loss of physical energy;
- Increase in thinking/mind speed, pulling bad memories;
- "Garbage" thoughts about death, dying, guilt, etc.
- Loss of sexual interest.

Emotional Memory files contain instructions for the brain to use these neurotransmitter ingredients to produce the mood in the file. We note that all anti-anxiety, antidepressant and antipsychotic medications focus on changing the levels of these chemicals in the brain.

Rule: Thoughts change brain chemistry.

That sounds so simple but that's the way it is, with our thoughts changing neurotransmitters on a daily basis. If a man walks into a room with a gun, we think "threat," and the brain releases nor epinephrine. We become tense, alert, develop sweaty palms and our heart beats faster. If he then bites the barrel of the gun, telling us the gun is actually chocolate, the brain rapids changes its opinion and we relax and laugh - the jokes on us.

We feel what we think! Positive thinking works. As the above example suggests, what we think about a situation actually creates our mood. Passed over for a promotion, we can either think we'll never get ahead in this job (lowering serotonin and making us depressed) or assume that we are being held back for another promotion or job transfer (makes a better mood).

Rule: The brain is constantly, every second, pulling files for our reference. It scans and monitors our environment constantly.

You've heard people compare the brain to a computer. Like a computer, the human brain has a huge database containing billions of files (memories) for our reference.

Always on the alert and ready to pull a file, the brain has built-in protection behaviours. People that are shy and introverted (socially uncomfortable and withdrawn) tell therapists that when they enter a restaurant, people look at them, creating anxiety. It's true. When anything enters our range of scanning, almost like our radar range, the brain looks at it. A person walking into a room is "scanned" by almost everyone else, that scanning procedure taking about two seconds. The brains looks: 1) to see if we have a file/reference and 2) for protection. If the new individual is odd-looking, carrying a weapon or naked - the brain will start a full-scan and react accordingly (long stare, fright or *"Don't I know you?"*)

Pulling these files automatically is great - unless they contain uncomfortable emotional memory. This is where another rule is important.

Rule: The emotional part of a memory begins 90 to 120 seconds after a file is pulled.

Once we pull a file, after 90 seconds the emotional component begins. Our mood starts to change, returning us to the mood, which was present when the file was made. As an example, remember someone discussing the recent death of a loved one. The first two minutes of conversation may go well - then they become sad. The longer the file is out (being discussed) the more the emotional component surfaces to the point that they will become tearful. If the file remains out, the exact feelings made at the time of the funeral and death will surface - they will talk about loss, love, guilt or whatever other feelings are in the file.

Socially, imagine having a "bad file" on an individual in the community. You are minding your own business. You turn the corner only to be confronted by Mr. X. What happens is this - your brain immediately pulls the file, you are somewhat confused at first and your emotion of anger, fear or whatever is in the file begins to surface. Even though you may not have seen the individual in 10 years, the Emotional Memory (EM) file is still active and wide-awake in your brain. This explains how many people can say that simply seeing an enemy or disliked person can ruin their entire day. If the file is not properly controlled, the mood will remain for the rest of the day.

The goal in file control is to prevent the 90 - second emotion from coming to the surface. We all have bad files but most people try to control them by preventing the emotional part from bothering them. They do this by putting the file away before the two-minute time limit.

Rule: The brain only allows one file out at a time.

This rule of brain operation is easy to understand. Much like a television, VCR or tape player, only one channel/program/tape is allowed to operate at a time. The brain works the same way.

As you read this paper, your brain is focusing on information in the paper. Luckily, the brain will focus on anything we choose or will play any file or tape we choose. If you suddenly decide to stop reading this paper and watch television, your brain will completely go along with that idea.

Also, your brain can switch files at the speed of light. As an example, allow your brain to change files as your read the following sentences:

1. Where was your best vacation?
2. Who is your favourite relative?
3. Think about the person who last died in your family.

As you read those questions, you brain immediately pulled the files to provide you with the information. The first two questions were rather routine and even if the files were allowed to remain open, would probably not cause much in the way of emotional distress or upset. However, what about the third file? If we allowed it to stay open, we may start thinking about departed grandmother, parents or close friends. That file, after the two-minute limit, would make us feel sad, lonely and create all the feelings associated with grief. Importantly, the brain doesn't care whether it's thinking about a departed relative or your favourite song.

Rule: The brain doesn't care which file is active.

Like the body, the brain operates many times on automatic. Our breathing operates the same way. We can take control of our breathing and inhale, exhale, inhale and so forth. We can also ignore our breathing, the brain will switch to automatic and we will breathe anyway.

The brain operates the same way. It will automatically pull files as we go about our day. As we see fellow co-workers, friends or neighbours, it will automatically pull their file - that's how we remember their name and information about them. The brain does this automatically. Importantly however, the brain really doesn't care which file is out. However, the fact that the brain operates on automatic is important to us.

When the brain operates on automatic, the files it pulls are greatly influenced by our mood. For example, if you are severely depressed, if your brain is left on "automatic," it will pull nothing but bad, trash and garbage files. When depressed, due to the brain chemistry involved, our brain will automatically pick bad files to torment us. Our brain will pull every bad file it can find, often far back into our childhood. As long as the depressed brain operates on automatic, it will continue to make us miserable by pulling every file, which has guilt, depression and a bad mood in it. It will play a series of our "worst hits."

Remember, we can change files at will. Since the brain really doesn't care which file is active, a depressed mood can be changed by simply switching the brain to manual, taking more control over our thoughts. This is especially helpful when a bad file is pulled accidentally.

Rule: Like the files, the brain only allows one feeling or emotion to be active at a time.

Again, this is a simple rule if we think about it. At any one second, the brain only allows one feeling. We cannot be happy and sad at the same time. As an example, it is almost impossible to be in a "romantic" mood if you are anxious, depressed or fearful. In another example, pull a file on someone you think is romantically attractive. Get a picture of that person in your mind. Now imagine someone throwing a large snake on your lap. You'll notice the romance immediately disappears and fear of the snake becomes the active emotion.

Many people have used this brain rule to deal with bad files. As an example, many people have bad files on certain individuals. Suppose we have a bad file on "John Doe." The mention of his name, seeing him in the street or any reference to this man brings up a bad file, which has bad feelings - anger, hatred, resentment, etc. One way to cope with this bad file is to place a funny name or comment on the file label. In other words, instead of a "John Doe" file, we now have a "Beanie Weenie" file. You'll notice that many divorced individuals have humorous names for their ex-spouse. This is the same principle. If we pull up a bad file but we have a funny name on it, it prolongs the emotion from surfacing and allows us to put the file away without any problem.

The fact that the brain allows only one feeling also allows us to have great control over our moods, more than we think. For example: A nasty neighbour calls and harasses us for some reason. We immediately pull the file on this neighbour, then another file as we are upset and end up hanging up with a mood of anger, resentment and an attitude of, *"I'll break her face."* As long as we keep her file out during the day, our mood will be the same - anger, resentment and so forth. In high stress jobs, for example, people frequently assure others that they don't take their job home with them, that they leave the work, briefcase and paperwork at the office. Importantly, while they don't take the "work" home with them, they clearly take the "mood" home with them. They don't bring home the briefcase, they bring home the irritability, tension and high-stress feelings.

However, if we choose to change our mood, we can do things like listen to favourite songs, look at a high school annual, look at vacation pictures and do other things, which will cause the brain to pull different files which have different moods - better moods.

Keep in mind, the brain will do anything we want: it will allow us to be angry the rest of the day or it will allow us to change its mood - it simply doesn't care.

Rule: You can't argue with a file.

When a file comes out, it is as though we have placed a tape in our VCR. The tape begins playing and we hear the same discussion or feel the same feelings over and over. Husbands and wives refer to this sometimes as "broken record" conversations. We get the same lectures, the same anger, the same resentment, the same everything - it's in the file. As an example, two people can be discussing whether they have enough money to purchase a lawnmower. The wife mentions using a particular credit card - that pulls a bad file in her husband, perhaps the "VISA" file. At that point, the husband launches into a long story about credit cards, high interest, harassing letters and so forth. When that file is opened up, a discussion about the lawnmower becomes useless.

The way files open and close in our brain can be a real problem with communication. While we may try to remain business-like and focus on a topic of discussion, we can't help but pull files. This brings up to another rule:

Rule: Any stimulation can pull a file.

Our body has five senses, vision, hearing, taste, touch and smell. A file can be pulled by any of those senses. An adult who has had a bad first marriage may automatically pull a jealousy file any time his wife mentions, *"I might be late."* The anxiety in that statement causes the brain to search for a file that makes sense - it pulls up a jealousy file from the first marriage. If the husband allows the file to stay out, he will become insecure, jealous and suspicious for no reason in the present. In second marriages, bad file pulling is a very common yet very hazardous activity.

Another common way that emotions pull files is in the case of a panic attack. When an individual suffers a panic attack, a powerful brain chemical is released in the frontal area of the brain, which creates the panic attack. After an attack however, we have clearly made a bad file - our brain remembers the attack and the feelings. Months later, we may be in a crowded store or in an emotionally tense situation when the brain recognises that emotion - it's seen it before during the panic attack. At that point, the brain immediately pulls the "panic attack" file. If we allow the file to stay out or pay attention to it, we are quite likely to have another panic attack - that's what's in the file.

Let's keep in mind that famous actors and actresses have known this method for years. If they want to cry on stage, they can pull a sensitive file from their personal life and within 90 seconds, tears are flowing. Remember: With each emotion or experience, the brain is always searching to see if we have a file on that topic.

A teenager who asks permission to go to the mall and is suddenly met with anger, resentment, accusations and suspiciousness by the parent - she has run into a severe communication block. Mother or dad has pulled a file from their teen years - a bad file. Again, we always know a file is out because the content or mood doesn't fit the present situation. We must then remember - you can't talk to a file. People who argue with the content of a file have as much chance as an individual who argues with the television while a videotape is playing.

Files and Depression

We have seen cases where patients have discussed a horrible experience from 15 to 20 years ago stating, *"I thought I got over it, I guess I didn't!"* Truthfully, they have gotten over that experience - but the file is still powerful. Depressed individuals suffer from the "garbage truck," that truckload of horrible files that prompt them to think about childhood trauma/abuse, previous relationships and rejections and any time they have failed within recollection. Again, the file makes us relive the emotions at that time. Even 20 years beyond the present, if we bring out a horrible file, we will feel horrible.

Clients that are depressed are encouraged not to pay attention to the various files being pulled. Again, when a depressed brain operates on automatic, it pulls nothing but garbage/trash. If you are depressed, be prepared to experience a tremendous amount of "mental garbage." Please, take no action on that garbage.

Files and Physical/Mental Trauma

One of the most common situations in which emotional memory files create severe problems is in physical or mental trauma. Trauma or severe emotional memory, can be created by physical assaults, combat experiences, crime, death of a loved one, viewing severe accidents, surgery or brush-with-death experiences.

If we are assaulted in our home, suddenly our home is no longer comfortable due to the memories it produces. A severe automobile accident may prompt people to quit driving completely or develop panic attacks if they near the site of the accident. Early sexual trauma, for example, can create poor sexual response/interest that will later affect marriages. Physical assault can produce problems with physical closeness many years later. Correction is often a matter of taking manual control of those situations, creating new files and "watering down" the old files.

Rule: The brain pulls the most recent and most powerful file first.

Imagine being stressed-out for six months, almost at the breaking point. You decide to stop by Kroger's to pick up some bread and milk. While in the store, you run into someone you dislike which immediately pulls a bad file. As you continue to see them in the store, you keep a file out and your mood becomes worse. At that point, your brain, already overtaxed, kicks in with a panic attack. You feel panicky, you begin to smother and you feel as though you are going to have a heart attack. You end up leaving your groceries and running out of the store.

You have thus created a panic-attack file with a label "Kroger" on it. Therefore, the next time you drive by Kroger's or stop for milk, your brain will pull the panic-attack file first. You'll develop a feeling - *"I can't go in there!"* Whenever we experience anxiety, the brain makes a file and includes the circumstances. This is exactly how people become agoraphobic - or become fearful of leaving their home. Several agoraphobic patients have areas of the town that are "off limits" - that area of the town pulls a panic file.

Dealing with Domestic Violence and Child Abuse

After a crisis or emotional upset, a file is made. If that file has a strong emotional value, it will be the first file pulled. Example: A relative by the name of Bill dies. For many months from that point, his death will be the first file pulled when anyone mentions the name. To avoid the constant reminder of sadness, when his name is mentioned we "skip" the first file and pull other "Bill" files, fishing trips, holidays with relatives, etc.

Techniques for File Control

1. Practice paying attention to how your file system works. If you find yourself in a bad mood or even happy mood, use the approach, *"What file is out?"* You will then find the file, what feeling is contained in the file and will then be able to have some control over the file.
2. If a bad file starts to come out, do something physical before the two-minute emotional release surfaces. If someone mentions a name or you have an event that brings up a bad file, for example, immediately pinch your ear, touch your watch or do something physical that lets you know a file is out. You may then change files mentally or even verbally. When talking with others, we can verbally change files by stating, *"That's kind of a sensitive topic for me. I'd rather not discuss that."* The physical action helps remind us that we have control over these files.
3. Take a bad file and put a funny name on it - the funnier the better. If we have people we dislike or even hate, a funny name is helpful in controlling the emotional content of that file. Common names that might be used are "Bozo," "Beanie Weenie," "Air Head," etc. It is also effective to combine both the funny name and physical action.
4. For example, if we call a gossip-oriented relative "Sinus Drip," we can combine the pulling of the file with the name and the physical action of blowing our nose. Again, as the brain will only allow one feeling at a time, the humour and physical action usually is enough to kill the file.
5. Many times we go through a series of horrible experiences, often lasting for years. These may include bad marriages, periods of unemployment, traumatic childhoods and so forth. Place all those files in one mental filing cabinet. Then place a label on the entire cabinet, one that reflects the condition at that time. Some clients have used such labels as, *"Wild and rowdy years," "My misery*

years," and so forth. When a file from that period is brought up, instead of focusing on the file and allowing the emotion to surface, the individual thinks to himself, *"That file is from my wild and rowdy years, it's not needed now."* Lumping all files together in one general category decreases the emotional impact and prevents pulling specific files.

6. Together with your spouse or significant other, you may train each other to recognise when one file is out. When a file pops out, a simple time-out hand signal, a certain look or a certain comment may make the other person aware that a file is out at the wrong time. This cuts down many arguments. Using this method, couples tend to stay on-track and discuss their concerns more at length, without being bothered by bad files.
7. Looks for "blocks" in communication with others. Often these emotional blocks are actually files being pulled in response to something the other person does. Do they sound like a relative/friend or do they remind you of something or some situation. Make a new file on that person.
8. Keep several good and mood-lifting files in close memory. If a bad file is pulled during the day, you then have good files ready to recall - and change your mood. Many people have files about vacation or other happy times to be used if a bad file is pulled. Always follow a bad file with a good file - it keeps your mood up.
9. In times of social crisis, create and rehearse a special file to cover uncomfortable questions - a "press release." During a divorce / separation situation, people frequently ask about your situation. Rather than pull up the "divorce" file, pull up a "divorce public relations" file that states *"things are pretty disorganised right now with us. I tell you more as things settle down."* Make the public relations file brief, short and sweet.
10. Practice file pulling, especially good files. Look at old pictures of happy times, high school yearbooks, etc. Observe the number of files that are pulled when you do this. It's amazing how much information your memory contains.

Rule: The Brain doesn't know if a file is real or imagined!

We have the ability to build our own files, even when the actual real-world experience is lacking. Using our imagination, we can alter files by imagining new information. If shy, we imagine ourselves in gradually more and more social situations, talking with friends, being in groups, giving talks to groups, teaching and finally being on Johnny Carson.

If we are wronged by someone, our anger becomes uncomfortable to the point that we begin imagining how guilty they must feel, how low their life really is and how they will be unhappy the rest of their days. After our brain works on that file, we eventually feel sorry for them! While the brain does this job for us normally, we need to hurry the process along at times.

Pick a target problem for improvement - then design, imagine and create a set of files to correct it.

Changing, Destroying and Contaminating Old Files

The brain's file system, just like the government's files, can be ruined and changed in many ways. One way to change a bad file is to alter its content, to add additional information of your choosing - again, the funnier the better. If you have a file where a parent is scolding you, bring up the file, then add the fact that the parent is only six inches tall, standing on a desk and shaking his/her little finger at you. We can also take a file, review the content and emotion and find funny things about the file. With some imagination, we can rewrite a file, which contained a fight or argument into something looking like The Three Stooges. If we put laughter/humour in the file, it changes the emotional content.

Files can also be "watered down." As an example, thinking about bad files while our favourite music plays in the background has a way of watering down a file, making it lose its emotional impact.

File Control in Special Situations

File control is a serious problem in alcohol or substance abuse. Remember: the alcohol and substance (marijuana, cocaine, etc.) automatically create good files due to their action on the brain. Sadly, bad files are created in the abusers home/family due to fights, arguments and hangovers. Therefore, thinking of alcohol/drugs rarely brings up a bad file to make the situation unpleasant. In fact, talking about drinking or using drugs usually brings a smile.

To combat this situation, those who have problems with drugs and/or alcohol are advised to pull a bad file when confronted with substances. This is a common situation in those trying to maintain sobriety. How many times have we socially heard someone turn down a beer with, *"No thanks. My wife would kill me! I'd have no job and my children wouldn't speak to me!"*

That person is using a file with a marital argument in it to kill his previous attraction to the substance. If people pulled up a file on their worst hangover every time they thought of alcohol, we might see a dramatic drop in national alcohol consumption.

Developing a Treatment Plan

Let's suppose we have a strong Emotional Memory (EM) perhaps the result of an automobile accident, a childhood trauma, a life-threatening experience, a physical assault, a public embarrassment or something equally emotionally traumatic. We can develop a treatment plan to eliminate the "emotional" part of the memory. We can never eliminate the details of the memory/experience - only brain damage or disease wipes out complete memories. The goal in the treatment of Emotional Memories (EM) is to eliminate the emotional component - the part that causes us emotional pain. If the emotional component/part is taken away, we can relate the story without fear of being upset or returning to that mood.

Keep in mind the goal with Emotional Memory (EM) - Eliminating the emotional part of the memory. One of the fastest and easiest ways to complete that task is to "water down" the emotional part of the memory. To do this, imagine having a letter saved on a computer word processor. Each time you retrieve the letter - it looks the same, reads the same and says the same thing. If we pull it up on the computer screen, read it, then save it - nothing has changed. This is what happens when we relate Emotional Memory (EM) events to others without adding to the memory or file.

What happens if we pull up that word processor letter each day? Each time we pull it up on the screen, we add one long sentence to the letter - a sentence that is silly, unrelated to the letter or just a bit off-base - then save it again. After two weeks we've added 14 sentences to the letter and the original letter is now gone. It's something totally different now. We use this technique to eliminate emotional parts of Emotional Memory (EM).

Technique: Each time we pull a bad Emotional Memory (EM) file, we add something to it; a comment, a joke, a physical gesture, etc. The brain will automatically save the file due to the new/added parts.

Sample Treatment Plan:

Event: We have been violently assaulted by someone.

Emotional part of the memory: The emotional component contains fears of dying, a fight-for-my-life feeling, panic and severe anxiety.

Procedure: Each time we bring up the Emotional Memory (EM) of the event, we add something - the funnier the better. For example: *"After that assault, I've cancelled my scheduled bout with Mike Tyson. I'm just not up to it."* Or, *"I've decided to market a line of assault-proof underwear. You think JC Penneys would be interested?"* Or, *"I've haven't had a fight like that since I used my brother's Beatles albums as Frisbees!"* It's like adding a sentence each time we review the word processor letter - watering down the original content over time.

We can make up or imagine part of the event as a humorous addition, for example *"I just kept thinking during the attack, my taxes are due!!"* The reactions of others to your humour will also be added to the file. This is why a World War II vet can talk calmly about horrible events during the war at the American Legion - he's discussed it so often, in so many different circumstances, that the emotional part has gone. Only the details remain. In Emotional Memory (EM) we naturally do this technique, commonly known as "getting over it." This paper just tells you how to do that faster and more efficiently. Any Emotional Memory (EM) can be approached in this manner and "watered down."

Conclusion:

However horrible the events are, victims can take charge of their lives and start to dispel their negative memories. They need to make their brain work for them rather than against them. Although this process requires constant vigilance, it becomes easier with constant practice.

"The Loser" - Warning Signs You're Dating a Loser

Very few relationships start on terms other than sweetness and politeness. In the beginning, "the honeymoon" of the relationship, it's difficult to determine what type of individual you are dating. Both you and the date are guarded, trying to obtain information about the other as much as possible without seeming like a police detective.

Romantic relationships can be wonderful with the right person. A relationship with the wrong individual however can lead to years of heartache, emotional/social damage and even physical damage. A damaging adult partner can damage us, damage our loved ones and even damage the way we feel about love and romance in the future.

They can turn what is supposed to be a loving, supporting and understanding relationship into the "fatal attraction" often described in movies. There are a variety of "bad choices" that may be encountered each week - most of which are easily to identify and avoid. We all know to avoid people that appear insane or abusive and not select them as a dating partner. However, some individuals are better at hiding their personality and behaviour abnormalities. In an effort to provide some warning about these very damaging individuals, this paper will outline a type of individual commonly found in the dating scene, a male or female labelled "The Loser".

"The Loser" is a type of partner that creates much social, emotional and psychological damage in a relationship. "The Loser" has permanent personality characteristics that create this damage. These are characteristics that they accept simply as the way they are and not a problem or psychological difficulty. In one sense, they have always lived with this personality and behaviour, often something they probably learned from their relatives/family. Psychologists usually treat the victims of "The Loser," women or men who arrive at the office severely depressed with their self-confidence and self-esteem totally destroyed.

The following list is an attempt to outline the characteristics of "The Loser" and provide a manner in which women and men can identify potentially damaging relationships before they are themselves severely damaged emotionally or even physically. If your partner possesses even one of these features, there is risk in the relationship. More than three of these indicators and you are involved with "The Loser" in a very high-risk relationship that will eventually create damage to you. When a high number of these features are present - it's not a probably or possibility. You will be hurt and damaged by "The Loser" if you stay in the relationship.

1. **Rough Treatment**: "The Loser" will hurt you on purpose. If s/he hits you, twists your arm, pulls your hair, kicks you, shoves you or breaks your personal property *even once*, drop him/her. Male losers often begin with behaviours that move you physically or hit the wall. Female losers often slap, kick and even punch their male partners when upset.

2. **Quick Attachment and Expression:** "The Loser" has very shallow emotions and connections with others. One of the things that might attract you to "The Loser" is how quickly s/he says, *"I love you,"* or wants to marry or commit to you. Typically, in less than a few weeks of dating you'll hear that you're the love of their life, they want to be with you forever and they want to marry you. You'll receive gifts, a variety of promises and be showered with their attention and nice gestures. This is the "honeymoon phase" - where they catch you and convince you that they are the best thing that ever happened to you.

   Remember the business saying, *"If it's too good to be true it probably is too good to be true!"* You may be so overwhelmed by this display of instant attraction, instant commitment and instant planning for the future that you'll miss the major point - it doesn't make sense!! Normal, healthy individuals require a long process to develop a relationship because there is so much at stake. Healthy individuals will wait for a lot of information before offering a commitment - not three weeks. It's true that we can become infatuated with others quickly - but not make such unrealistic promises and have the future planned after three dates. The rapid warm-up is always a sign of shallow emotions which later cause "The Loser" to detach from you as quickly as they committed. "The Loser" typically wants to move in with you or marry you in less than four weeks or very early in the relationship.

3. **Frightening Temper**: "The Loser" has a scary temper. If your boyfriend or girlfriend blows up and does dangerous things, like driving too fast because they're mad, breaking/throwing things, getting into fights or threatening others - that temper will soon be turned in your direction. In the beginning of the relationship, you will be exposed to "witnessed violence" - fights with others, threats toward others, angry outbursts at others, etc. You will also hear of violence in their life. You will see and witness this temper - throwing things, yelling, cursing, driving fast, hitting the walls and kicking things. That quickly serves to intimidate you and fear their potential for violence, although

   "The Loser" quickly assures you that they are angry at others or situations, not at you. At first, you will be assured that they will never direct the hostility and violence at you - but they are clearly letting you know that they have that ability and capability - and that it might come your way. Later, you fear challenging or confronting them - fearing that same temper and violence will be turned in your direction.

4. **Killing Your Self-Confidence**: "The Loser" repeatedly puts you down. They constantly correct your slight mistakes, making you feel "on guard," unintelligent and leaving you with the feeling that you are always doing something wrong. They tell you that you're too fat, too unattractive or don't talk correctly or look well. This gradual chipping away at your confidence and self-esteem allows them to later treat you badly - as though you deserved it. In public, you will be "walking on eggshells" - always fearing you are doing or saying something that will later create a temper outburst or verbal argument.

5. **Cutting Off Your Support**: In order to control someone completely, you must cut off their supportive friends - sometimes even their family. "The Loser" feels your friends and family might influence you or offer negative opinions about their behaviour. "The Loser" begins by telling you these friends treat you badly, take advantage of you and don't understand the special nature of the love you share with them. In some cases, if they can't get rid of your best same-sex friend, "The Loser" will claim s/he made a pass at them. If you talk to your friends or family, "The Loser" will punish you by asking multiple questions or making nasty accusations.

Eventually, rather than face the verbal punishment, interrogation and abuse, you'll develop the feeling that it's better not to talk to family and friends. You will withdraw from friends and family, prompting them to become upset with you. "The Loser" then tells you they are treating you badly again and you'd be better to keep your distance from them. Once you are isolated and alone, without support, their control over you can increase.

6. **The Mean and Sweet Cycle:** "The Loser" cycles from mean to sweet and back again. The cycle starts when they are intentionally hurtful and mean. You may be verbally abused, cursed and threatened over something minor. Suddenly, the next day they become sweet, doing all those little things they did when you started dating. You hang on; hoping each mean-then-sweet cycle is the last one. The other purpose of the mean cycle is to allow "The Loser" to say very nasty things about you or those you care about, again chipping away at your self-esteem and self-confidence. "The

Loser" often apologises but the damage to your self-esteem is already done - exactly as planned.

7. **It's Always Your Fault:** "The Loser" blames you for his/her anger as well as any other behaviour that is incorrect. When s/he cheats on you, yells at you, treats you badly, damages your property or embarrasses you publicly - it's somehow your fault. If you are ten minutes late for a date, it's your fault that the male loser drives 80 miles per hour, runs people off the road and pouts the rest of the evening. "The Loser" tells you his/her anger and misbehaviour would not have happened if you had not made some simple mistake, had loved them more or had not questioned his/her behaviour.

   "The Loser" never, repeats never takes personal responsibility for his/her behaviour - it's always the fault of someone else. If he drives like a maniac and tries to pull an innocent driver off the highway to assault them - it's actually the fault of the other driver (not his) as he didn't use a turn signal when he changed lanes. S/he gives you the impression that you had it (anger, yelling, assault) coming and deserved the anger, violence, pouting or physical display of aggression.

8. **Break-up Panic**: "The Loser" panics at the idea of breaking up - unless it's totally his/her idea - then you're dropped like a hot rock. Abusive boyfriends often break down and cry, they plead, they promise to change and they offer marriage/trips/gifts when you threaten ending the relationship. Both male and female losers may threaten suicide, threaten to return to old sweethearts (who feel lucky they're gone!) or threaten to quit their job and leave the area - as though you will be responsible for those decisions. "The Loser" offers a multitude of "deals" and halfway measures, like *"Let's just date one more month!"*

   They shower you with phone calls, often every five minutes, hoping that you will make an agreement or see them just to stop the telephone harassment. Some call your relatives, your friends, their friends and anyone else they can think of - telling those people to call you and tell you how much they love you.

   Creative losers often create so much social pressure that the victim agrees to go back to the bad relationship rather than continue under the social pressure. Imagine trying to end a relationship and receiving tearful calls from all his/her relatives (they secretly hope you'll keep him/her so they don't have to) seeing a plea for your return in the newspaper or even on a local billboard, receiving flowers at work each day or having him/her arrive at your place of work and offer you a wedding ring (male loser technique) or inform you that they might be pregnant (female loser technique) in front of your co-workers! Their reaction is emotionally intense; a behaviour they use to keep you an emotional prisoner.

If you go back to them, you actually fear a worse reaction if you threaten to leave again (making you a prisoner) and they later frequently recall the incident to you as further evidence of what a bad person you are. Remember, if your prize dog jumps the fence and escapes, if you get him back you build a higher fence. Once back in the grasp of "The Loser" - escape will be three times as difficult the next time.

9. **No Outside Interests**: "The Loser" will encourage you to drop your hobbies, interests and involvement with others. If you have an individual activity, they demand that they accompany you, making you feel miserable during the entire activity. The idea behind this is to prevent you from having fun or interests other than those that they totally control.

10. **Paranoid Control**: "The Loser" will check up on you and keep track of where you are and whom you are with. If you speak to a member of the opposite sex, you receive twenty questions about how you know them. If you don't answer their phone call, they are asking where you were, what were you doing, who you were talking to, etc. They will notice the type of mud on your car, question why you shop certain places and question why you called a friend, why the friend called you and so forth. Some losers follow you to the grocery and then later ask if you've been there in an attempt to catch you in a lie. In severe cases, they go through your mail, look through your purse / wallet, hit your redial on the phone when they arrive or search through your garbage for evidence.

High-tech losers may encourage you to make "private" calls to friends from their residence, calls that are being secretly taped for later reference. They may begin to tell you what to wear, what music to listen to and how to behave in public. Eventually, they tell you that you can not talk to certain friends or acquaintances, go certain places or talk about certain issues in public. If no date is present on Friday night - "The Loser" will inform you that they will call you that night - sometime. That effectively keeps you home, awaiting the call, fearing the verbal abuse and questions you might receive if you weren't home for the call. This technique allows "The Loser" to do what they want socially, at the same time controlling your behaviour from a distance or a local bar.

11. **Public Embarrassment**: In an effort to keep you under control while in public, "The Loser" will lash out at you, call you names or say cruel or embarrassing things about you in private or in front of people. When in public, you quickly learn that any opinion you express may cause them to verbally attack you, either at the time or later. If you stay with "The Loser" too long, you'll soon find yourself politely smiling, saying nothing and holding on to their arm when in public. You'll also find yourself walking with your head down, fearful of seeing a friend who might speak to you and create an angry reaction in "The Loser".

12. **It's Never Enough**: "The Loser" convinces you that you are never quite good enough. You don't say *"I love you"* enough, you don't stand close enough, you don't do enough for them after all their sacrifices and your behaviour always falls short of what is expected. This is another method of destroying your self-esteem and confidence. After months of this technique, they begin telling you how lucky you are to have them - somebody who tolerates someone as inadequate and worthless as you.

13. **Entitlement**: "The Loser" has a tremendous sense of entitlement, the attitude that they have a perfectly logical right to do whatever they desire. If cut off in traffic, "The Loser" feels they have the right to run the other driver off the road, assault them and endanger the lives of other drivers with their temper tantrum. Keep in mind; this same sense of entitlement will be used against you. If you disobey their desires or demands or violate one of their rules, they feel they are entitled to punish you in any manner they see fit.

14. **Your Friends and Family Dislike Him:** As the relationship continues; your friends and family will see what "The Loser" is doing to you. They will notice a change in your personality or your withdrawal. They will protest. "The Loser" will tell you they are jealous of the "special love" you have and then use their protest and opinion as further evidence that they are against you - not him. The mention of your family members or friends will spark an angry response from them - eventually placing you in the situation where you stop talking about those you care about, even your own family members. "The Loser" will be jealous and threatened by

anyone you are close to - even your children. In some cases, your parents or brothers/sisters will not be allowed to visit your home.

15. **Bad Stories**: People often let you know about their personality by the stories they tell about themselves. It's the old story about giving a person enough rope and they'll hang themselves. The stories a person tells informs us of how they see themselves, what they think is interesting and what they think will impress you. A humorous individual will tell funny stories on himself. "The Loser" tells stories of violence, aggression, being insensitive to others, rejecting others, etc. They may tell you about past relationships and in every case; they assure you that they were treated horribly despite how wonderful they were to that person.

    They brag about their temper and outbursts because they don't see anything wrong with violence and actually take pride in the, *"I don't take nothing from nobody"* attitude. People define themselves with their stories, much like a culture is described by its folklore and legends. Listen to these stories - they tell you how you will eventually be treated and what's coming your way.

16. **The Waitress Test**: It's been said that when dating, the way an individual treats a waitress or other neutral person of the opposite sex is the way they will treat you in six months. During the "honeymoon phase" of a relationship, you will be treated like a king or queen. However, during that time "The Loser" has not forgotten how s/he basically feels about the opposite sex. Waitresses, clerks or other neutral individuals will be treated badly. If they are cheap - you'll never receive anything once the honeymoon is over. If they whine, complain, criticise and torment - that's how they'll treat you in six months. A mentally healthy person is consistent; they treat almost all people the same way all the time. If you find yourself dating a man who treats you like a queen and other females like dirt - hit the road.

17. **The Reputation**: As mentioned, mentally healthy individuals are consistent in their personality and their behaviour. "The Loser" may have two distinct reputations - a group of individuals who will give you glowing reports and a group that will warn you that they are serious trouble. If you ask ten people about a new restaurant - five say it's wonderful and five say it's a hog pit - you clearly understand that there's some risk involved in eating there. "The

Loser" may actually brag about their reputation as a "butt kicker," "womaniser," "hot temper," or "being crazy."

They may tell you stories where others have called them crazy or suggested that they receive professional help. Pay attention to the reputation. Reputation is the public perception of an individual's behaviour. If the reputation has two sides, good and bad, your risk is high. You will be dealing with the bad side once the honeymoon is over in the relationship. With severe behaviour problems, "The Loser" will be found to have almost no friends, just acquaintances. Emotionally healthy and moral individuals will not tolerate friendships with losers that treat others so badly. If you find yourself disliking the friends of "The Loser," it's because they operate the same way they do and you can see it in them.

18. **Walking on Eggshells**: As a relationship with "The Loser" continues, you will gradually be exposed to verbal intimidation, temper tantrums, lengthy interrogations about trivial matters, violence/threats directed at others but witnessed by you, paranoid preoccupation with your activities and a variety of put-downs on your character. You will quickly find yourself "walking on eggshells" in their presence - fearful to bring up topics, fearful to mention that you spoke to or saw a friend and fearful to question or criticise the behaviour of "The Loser." Instead of experiencing the warmth and comfort of love, you will be constantly on edge, tense when talking to others (they might say something that you'll have to explain later) and fearful that you'll see someone you'll have to greet in public. Dates and times together will be more comfortable and less threatening when totally alone - exactly what "The Loser" wants - no interference with their control or dominance.

19. **Discounted Feelings/Opinions**: "The Loser" is so self-involved and self-worshiping that the feelings and opinions of others are considered worthless. As the relationship continues and you begin to question what you are feeling or seeing in their behaviour, you will be told that your feelings and opinions don't make sense, they're silly and that you are emotionally disturbed to even think of such things. "The Loser" has no interest in your opinion or your feelings - but they will be disturbed and upset that you dare question their behaviour. "The Loser" is extremely hostile toward criticism and often reacts with anger or rage when their behaviour is questioned.

20. **They Make You "Crazy:"** "The Loser" operates in such a damaging way that you find yourself doing "crazy" things in self-defence. If "The Loser" is scheduled to arrive at 8:00 pm - you call Time & Temperature to cover the redial, check your garbage for anything that might get you in trouble and call your family and friends to tell them not to call you that night. You warn family/friends not to bring up certain topics, avoid locations in the community where you might see co-workers or friends and not speak to others for fear of the 20 questions. You become paranoid as well - being careful what you wear and say.

Non-violent males find themselves in physical fights with female losers. Non-violent females find themselves yelling and screaming when they can no longer take the verbal abuse or intimidation. In emotional and physical self-defence, we behave differently and oddly. While we think we are "going crazy" - it's important to remember that there is no such thing as "normal behaviour" in a combat situation. Rest assured that your behaviour will return to normal if you detach from "The Loser" before permanent psychological damage is done.

Dangerous Versions of "The Loser"

There are more severe if not dangerous versions of "The Loser" that have been identified over the years. If you are involved in a relationship with one of these versions, you may require professional and legal assistance to save yourself.

Physical Abuser: Physical abusers begin the relationship with physical moving - shoving, pushing, forcing, etc. That quickly moves into verbal threats with physical gestures - the finger in the face, clinched fist in the face and voiced physical threats such as, *"You make me want to break your face!"* Eventually, these combine to form actual physical abuse - hitting, slapping and kicking. "The Loser" is always sorry the next day and begins the mean-then-sweet cycle all over again. Getting away from physical abusers often requires the assistance of family, law enforcement agencies or local abuse agencies. Female losers often physically attack their partner, break car windows or behave with such violence that the male partner is forced to physically protect himself from the assault. If the female loser is bruised in the process of self-protection, as when physically restraining her from hitting, those bruises are then "displayed" to others as evidence of what a bad person the partner is and how abusive they have been in the relationship.

Psychotic Losers: There are losers that are severely ill in a psychiatric sense - the movie description of the "Fatal Attraction." Some may tell you wild stories and try to convince you that they are connected to The Mob or a government agency (CIA, FBI, etc.). They may fake terminal illness, pregnancy or disease. They intimidate and frighten you with comments such as, *"I can have anyone killed ..."* or *"No one leaves a relationship with me ..."*

If you try to end the relationship, they react violently and give you the impression that you, your friends or your family are in serious danger. People often then remain in the abusive and controlling relationship due to fear of harm to their family or their reputation. While such fears are unrealistic as "The Loser" is only interested in controlling you, those fears feel very real when combined with the other characteristics of "The Loser."

Psychotic or psychiatrically ill losers may also stalk, follow or harass you. They may threaten physical violence, show weapons or threaten to kill you or themselves if you leave them. If you try to date others, they may follow you or threaten your new date. Your new date may be subjected to phone harassment, vandalism, threats and even physical assaults. If you are recently divorced, separated or recently ended another relationship, "The Loser" may be intimidating toward your ex-partner, fearing you might return if the other partner is not "scared off.' Just remember - everything "The Loser" has ever done to anyone will be coming your way. "The Loser" may send you pictures of you, your children or your family - pictures they have taken secretly - hinting that they can "reach out and touch" those you love. You may need help and legal action to separate from these individuals.

Guidelines for Detachment

Separating from "The Loser" often involves three stages: The Detachment, Ending the Relationship and the Follow-up Protection.

The Detachment

During this part of separating from "The Loser," you recognise what you must do and create an Exit Plan. Many individuals fail in attempts to detach from "The Loser" because they leave suddenly and

Dealing with Domestic Violence and Child Abuse

impulsively, without proper planning and without resources. In many cases, "The Loser" has isolated their partner from others, has control of finances or has control of major exit needs such as an automobile. During the detachment phase you should ...

- Observe the way you are treated. Watch for the methods listed above and see how "The Loser" works.
- Gradually become more boring, talk less and share less feelings and opinions. The goal is almost to bore "The Loser" to lessen the emotional attachment, at the same time not creating a situation which would make you a target.
- Quietly contact your family and supportive others. Determine what help they might be - a place to stay, protection, financial help, etc.
- If you fear violence or abuse, check local legal or law enforcement options such as a restraining order.
- If "The Loser" is destructive, slowly move your valuables from the home if together or try to recover valuables if in their possession. In many cases, you may lose some personal items during your detachment - a small price to pay to get rid of "The Loser".
- Stop arguing, debating or discussing issues. Stop defending and explaining yourself - responding with comments such as, *"I've been so confused lately" or "I'm under so much stress I don't know why I do anything anymore."*
- Begin dropping hints that you are depressed, burned out or confused about life in general. Remember - "The Loser" never takes responsibility for what happens in any relationship. "The Loser" will feel better about leaving the relationship if they can blame it on you. Many individuals are forced to "play confused" and dull, allowing "The Loser" to tell others, *"My girlfriend's (or boyfriend's) about half nuts!"* They may tell others you're crazy or confused but you'll be safer. Allow them to think anything they want about you as long as you're in the process of detaching.
- Don't start another relationship. That will only complicate your situation and increase the anger. Your best bet is to "lay low" for several months. Remember, "The Loser" will quickly locate another victim and become instantly attached as long as the focus on you is allowed to die down.
- As "The Loser" starts to question changes in your behaviour, admit confusion, depression, emotionally numbness and a host of other

boring reactions. This sets the foundation for the ending of the relationship.

Ending the Relationship

Remembering that "The Loser" doesn't accept responsibility, responds with anger to criticism and is prone to panic detachment reactions - ending the relationship continues the same theme as the detachment.

Explain that you are emotionally numb, confused and burned out. You can't feel anything for anybody and you want to end the relationship almost for his/her benefit. Remind them that they've probably noticed something is wrong and that you need time to sort out your feelings and fix whatever is wrong with you. As disgusting as it may seem, you may have to use a theme of, *"I'm not right for anyone at this point in my life."* If "The Loser" can blame the end on you, as they would if they ended the relationship anyway, they will depart faster.

If "The Loser" panics, you'll receive a shower of phone calls, letters, notes on your car, etc. React to each in the same manner with a boring *'thanks.'* If you overreact or give in, you've lost control again.

Focus on your need for time away from the situation. Don't agree to the many negotiations that will be offered - dating less frequently, dating only once a week, taking a break for only a week, going to counselling together, etc. As long as "The Loser" has contact with you they feel there is a chance to manipulate you.

"The Loser" will focus on making you feel guilty. In each phone contact you'll hear how much you are loved, how much was done for you and how much they have sacrificed for you. At the same time, you'll hear about what a bum you are for leading them on, not giving them an opportunity to fix things and embarrassing them by ending the relationship.

Don't try to make them understand how you feel - it won't happen. "The Loser" only is concerned with how they feel - your feelings are irrelevant. You will be wasting your time trying to make them understand and they will see the discussions as an opportunity to make you feel guiltier and manipulate you.

Don't fall for sudden changes in behaviour or promises of marriage, trips, gifts, etc. By this time you have already seen how "The Loser" is normally and naturally. While anyone can change for a short period of time, they always return to their normal behaviour once the crisis is over.

Seek professional counselling for yourself or the support of others during this time. You will need encouragement and guidance. Keep in mind; if "The Loser" finds out you are seeking help they will criticise the counselling, the therapist or the effort.

Don't use terms like "someday," "maybe," or "in the future." When "The Loser" hears such possibilities, they think you are weakening and will increase their pressure.

Imagine a dead slot machine. If we are in Las Vegas at a slot machine and pull the handle ten times and nothing happens - we move on to another machine. However, if on the tenth time the slot machine pays us even a little, we keep pulling the handle - thinking the jackpot is on the way. If we are very stern and stable about the decision to end the relationship over many days, then suddenly offer a possibility or hope for reconciliation - we've given a little pay and the pressure will continue. Never change your position - always say the same thing. "The Loser" will stop playing a machine that doesn't pay off and quickly move to another.

Follow-up Protection

"The Loser" never sees their responsibility or involvement in the difficulties in the relationship. From a psychological standpoint, "The Loser" has lived and behaved in this manner most of their life, clearly all of their adult life. As they really don't see themselves at fault or as an individual with a problem, "The Loser" tends to think that the girlfriend or boyfriend is simply going through a phase - their partner (victim) might be temporarily mixed up or confused, they might be listening to the wrong people or they might be angry about something and will get over it soon. "The Loser" rarely detaches completely and will often try to continue contact with the partner even after the relationship is terminated. During the Follow-up Protection period, some guidelines are:

- Never change your original position. It's over permanently! Don't talk about possible changes in your position in the future. You might think that will calm "The Loser" but it only tells them that the possibilities still exist and only a little more pressure is needed to return to the relationship.

- Don't agree to meetings or reunions to discuss old times. For "The Loser," discussing old times is actually a way to upset you, put you off guard and use the guilt to hook you again.
- Don't offer details about your new life or relationships. Assure him that both his life and your life are now private and that you hope they are happy.
- If you start feeling guilty during a phone call, get off the phone fast. More people return to bad marriages and relationships due to guilt than anything else. If you listen to those phone calls, as though taping them, you'll find "The Loser" spends most of the call trying to make you feel guilty.
- In any contact with the ex "Loser," provide only a status report, much like you'd provide to your Aunt Gladys. For example: *"I'm still working hard and not getting any better at tennis. That's about it."*
- When "The Loser" tells you how difficult the break-up has been, share with him some general thoughts about breaking-up and how finding the right person is difficult. While "The Loser" wants to focus on your relationship, talk in terms of Ann Landers - *"Well, breaking up is hard on anyone. Dating is tough in these times. I'm sure we'll eventually find someone that's right for both of us."* Remember - nothing personal!
- Keep all contact short and sweet - the shorter the better. As far as "The Loser" is concerned, you're always on your way somewhere, there's something in the microwave or your mother is walking up the steps to your home. Wish "The Loser" well but always with the same tone of voice that you might offer to someone you have just talked to at the grocery store. For phone conversations, electronic companies make a handy gadget that produces about twenty sounds - a doorbell, an oven or microwave alarm, a knock on the door, etc. That little device is handy to use on the phone - the microwave dinner just came out or someone is at the door. Do whatever you have to do to keep the conversation short - and not personal.

Conclusion:

'Losers' can actually be easily identified. However attached you may be, once you notice the signs, resolve to get out and follow through on your resolve. Use the steps outlined earlier as your guide. As you do so, ensure you have a strong support group – those who were likely your close friends before you met 'the loser.'

Love and the Stockholm Syndrome: The Mystery of Loving an Abuser

In clinical practice, some of the most surprised and shocked individuals are those who have been involved in controlling and abusive relationships. When the relationship ends, they offer comments such as, *"I know what he's done to me, but I still love him,"* *"I don't know why, but I want him back,"* or *"I know it sounds crazy, but I miss her."* Recently I've heard, *"This doesn't make sense. He's got a new girlfriend and he's abusing her too ... but I'm jealous!"*

Friends and relatives are even more amazed and shocked when they hear these comments or witness their loved one returning to an abusive relationship. While the situation doesn't make sense from a social stand-point, does it make sense from a psychological viewpoint? The answer is - Yes!

On August 23rd, 1973 two machine-gun carrying criminals entered a bank in Stockholm, Sweden. Blasting their guns, one prison escapee named Jan-Erik Olsson announced to the terrified bank employees, *"The party has just begun!"* The two bank robbers held four hostages, three women and one man, for the next 131 hours. The hostages were strapped with dynamite and held in a bank vault until finally rescued on August 28th.

After their rescue, the hostages exhibited a shocking attitude considering they were threatened, abused and feared for their lives for over five days. In their media interviews, it was clear that they supported their captors and actually feared law enforcement personnel who came to their rescue. The hostages had begun to feel the captors were actually protecting them from the police. One woman later became engaged to one of the criminals and another developed a legal defence fund to aid in their criminal defence fees. Clearly, the hostages had "bonded" emotionally with their captors.

While the psychological condition in hostage situations became known as "Stockholm Syndrome" due to the publicity - the emotional "bonding" with captors was a familiar story in psychology. It had been recognised many years before and was found in studies of other hostage, prisoner or abusive situations such as:

- Abused Children;
- Battered/Abused Women;
- Prisoners of War;
- Cult Members;
- Incest Victims;
- Criminal Hostage Situations;
- Concentration Camp Prisoners;
- Controlling/Intimidating Relationships.

In the final analysis, emotionally bonding with an abuser is actually a strategy for survival for victims of abuse and intimidation. The "Stockholm Syndrome" reaction in hostage and/or abuse situations is so well recognised at this time that police hostage negotiators no longer view it as unusual. In fact, it is often encouraged in crime situations as it improves the chances for survival of the hostages. On the down side, it also assures that the hostages experiencing "Stockholm Syndrome" will not be very cooperative during rescue or criminal prosecution.

Local law enforcement personnel have long recognised this syndrome with battered women who fail to press charges, bail their battering husband/boyfriend out of jail and even physically attack police officers when they arrive to rescue them from a violent assault.

Stockholm Syndrome (SS) can also be found in family, romantic and interpersonal relationships. The abuser may be a husband or wife, boyfriend or girlfriend, father or mother or any other role in which the abuser is in a position of control or authority.

Every syndrome has symptoms or behaviours and Stockholm Syndrome is no exception. While a clear-cut list has not been established due to varying opinions by researchers and experts, several of these features will be present:

- Positive feelings by the victim toward the abuser/controller;
- Negative feelings by the victim toward family, friends or authorities trying to rescue/support them or win their release;
- Support of the abuser's reasons and behaviours;
- Positive feelings by the abuser toward the victim;
- Supportive behaviours by the victim, at times helping the abuser;
- Inability to engage in behaviours that may assist in their release or detachment.

Stockholm Syndrome doesn't occur in every hostage or abusive situation. In another bank robbery involving hostages, after terrorising patrons and employees for many hours, a police sharpshooter shot and wounded the terrorising bank robber. After he hit the floor, two women picked him up and physically held him up to the window for another shot. As you can see, the length of time one is exposed to abuse/control and other factors are certainly involved.

It has been found that four situations or conditions are present that serve as a foundation for the development of Stockholm Syndrome. These four situations can be found in hostage, severe abuse and abusive relationships:

- The presence of a perceived threat to one's physical or psychological survival and the belief that the abuser would carry out the threat;
- The presence of a perceived small kindness from the abuser to the victim;
- Isolation from perspectives other than those of the abuser;
- The perceived inability to escape the situation.
- By considering each situation we can understand how Stockholm Syndrome develops in romantic relationships as well as criminal/hostage situations. Looking at each situation:

Perceived Threat to One's Physical/Psychological Survival

Criminal or antisocial partners can directly threaten your life or the life of friends and family. Their history of violence leads us to believe that the captor/controller will carry out the threat in a direct manner if we fail to comply with their demands. The abuser assures us that only our co-operation keeps our loved ones safe.

Indirectly, the abuser/controller offers subtle threats that you will never leave them or have another partner, reminding you that people in the past have paid dearly for not following their wishes. Hints are often offered such as, *"I know people who can make others disappear."* Indirect threats also come from the stories told by the abuser or controller - how they obtained revenge on those who have crossed them in the past. These stories of revenge are told to remind the victim that revenge is possible if they leave.

Witnessing violence or aggression is also a perceived threat. Witnessing a violent temper directed at a television set, others on the highway or a third party clearly sends us the message that we could be the next targets for violence. Witnessing the thoughts and attitudes of the abuser/controller is threatening and intimidating, knowing that we will be the targets of those thoughts in the future.

The "Small Kindness" Perception

In threatening and survival situations, we look for evidence of hope - a small sign that the situation may improve. When an abuser/controller shows the victim some small kindness, even though it is to the abusers benefit as well, the victim interprets that small kindness as a positive trait of the captor. In criminal/war hostage situations, letting the victim live is often enough. Small behaviours, such as allowing a bathroom visit or providing food/water, are enough to strengthen the Stockholm Syndrome in criminal hostage events.

In relationships with abusers, a birthday card, a gift (usually provided after a period of abuse) or a special treat are interpreted as not only positive, but evidence that the abuser is not "all bad" and may at some time correct his/her behaviour. Abusers and controllers are often given positive credit for not abusing their partner, when the partner would have normally been subjected to verbal or physical abuse in a certain situation. An aggressive and jealous partner may normally become intimidating or abusive in certain social situations, as when an opposite-sex co-worker waves in a crowd. After seeing the wave, the victim expects to be verbally battered and when it doesn't happen, that "small kindness" is interpreted as a positive sign.

Similar to the small kindness perception is the perception of a "soft side." During the relationship, the abuser/controller may share information about his/her past - how s/he was mistreated, abused, neglected or wronged. The victim begins to feel the abuser/controller may be capable of fixing his/her behaviour or worse yet, that s/he (abuser) may also be a "victim." Sympathy may develop toward the abuser and we often hear the victim of Stockholm Syndrome defending their abuser with, *"I know he fractured my jaw and ribs ... but he's troubled. He had a rough childhood!"*

Losers and abusers may admit they need psychiatric help or acknowledge they are mentally disturbed; however, it's almost always after they have already abused or intimidated the victim. The admission is a way of denying responsibility for the abuse. In truth, personality disorders and criminals have learned over the years that personal responsibility for their violent/abusive behaviours can be minimised and even denied by blaming their bad upbringing, abuse as a child and now - video games. One murderer blamed his crime on eating too much junk food - now known as the "Twinkie Defence." While it may be true that the abuser/controller had a difficult upbringing - showing sympathy for his/her history produces no change in his/her behaviour and in fact, prolongs the length of time you will be abused. While "sad stories" are always included in their apologies - after the abusive / controlling event - their behaviour never changes! Keep in mind; once you become hardened to the "sad stories," they will simply try another approach. I know of no victim of abuse or crime who has heard his/her abuser say, *"I'm beating (robbing, mugging, etc.) you because my Mom hated me!"*

Isolation from Perspectives Other than those of the Captor

In abusive and controlling relationships, the victim has the sense they are always "walking on eggshells" - fearful of saying or doing anything that might prompt a violent/intimidating outburst. For their survival, they begin to see the world through the abuser's perspective. They begin to fix things that might prompt an outburst, act in ways they know makes the abuser happy or avoid aspects of their own life that may prompt a problem. If we only have a dollar in our pocket, then most of our decisions become financial decisions. If our partner is an abuser or controller, then the majority of our decisions are based on our perception of the abuser's potential reaction. We become preoccupied with the needs, desires and habits of the abuser/controller.

Taking the abuser's perspective as a survival technique can become so intense that the victim actually develops anger toward those trying to help them. The abuser is already angry and resentful toward anyone who would provide the victim support, typically using multiple methods and manipulations to isolate the victim from others. Any contact the victim has with supportive people in the community is met with accusations, threats and/or violent outbursts. Victims then turn on their family - fearing family contact will cause additional violence and abuse in the home.

At this point, victims curse their parents and friends, tell them not to call and stop interfering and break off communication with others. Agreeing with the abuser/controller, supportive others are now viewed as "causing trouble" and must be avoided. Many victims threaten their family and friends with restraining orders if they continue to "interfere" or try to help the victims in their situation. On the surface it would appear that they have sided with the abuser/controller. In truth, they are trying to minimise contact situation that might make them a target of additional verbal abuse or intimidation. If a casual phone call from Mom prompts a two-hour temper outburst with threats and accusations - the victim quickly realises it's safer if Mom stops calling. If simply telling Mom to stop calling doesn't work, for his/her own safety the victim may accuse Mom of attempting to ruin the relationship and demand that she stop calling.

In severe cases of Stockholm Syndrome in relationships, the victim may have difficulty leaving the abuser and may actually feel the abusive situation is their fault. In law enforcement situations, the victim may actually feel the arrest of their partner for physical abuse or battering is their fault. Some women will allow their children to be removed by child protective agencies rather than give up the relationship with their abuser. As they take the perspective of the abuser, the children are at fault - they complained about the situation, they brought the attention of authorities to the home and they put the adult relationship at risk. Sadly, the children have now become a danger to the victim's safety. For those with Stockholm Syndrome, allowing the children to be removed from the home decreases their victim's stress while providing an emotionally and physically safer environment for the children.

Perceived Inability to Escape

As a hostage in a bank robbery, threatened by criminals with guns, it's easy to understand the perceived inability to escape. In romantic relationships, the belief that one can't escape is also very common. Many abusive/controlling relationships feel like till-death-do-us-part relation-ships - locked together by mutual financial issues/assets, mutual intimate knowledge or legal situations. Here are some common situations:

- Controlling partners have increased the financial obligations/debt in the relationship to the point that neither partner can financially survive on his/her own.
- Controllers who sense their partner may be leaving will often purchase a new automobile, later claiming they can't pay alimony or child support due to their large car payments.
- The legal ending of a relationship, especially a martial relation-ship, often creates significant problems. A Controller who has an

income that is "under the table" or maintained through legally questionable situations runs the risk of those sources of income being investigated or made public by the divorce/separation. The Controller then becomes more agitated about the possible public exposure of their business arrangements than the loss of the relationship.
- The Controller often uses extreme threats including threatening to take the children out of state, threatening to quit their job/business rather than pay alimony/support, threatening public exposure of the victim's personal issues or assuring the victim they will never have a peaceful life due to non-stop harassment. In severe cases, the Controller may threaten an action that will undercut the victim's support such as, *"I'll see that you lose your job"* or *"I'll have your automobile burned."*
- Controllers often keep the victim locked into the relationship with severe guilt - threatening suicide if the victim leaves. The victim hears, *"I'll kill myself in front of the children," "I'll set myself on fire in the front yard,"* or *"Our children won't have a father/mother if you leave me!"*

In relationships with an abuser or controller, the victim has also experienced a loss of self-esteem, self-confidence and psychological energy. The victim may feel "burned out" and too depressed to leave. Additionally, abusers and controllers often create a type of dependency by controlling the finances, placing automobiles/ homes in their name and eliminating any assets or resources the victim may use to leave. In clinical practice I've heard, *"I'd leave but I can't even get money out of the savings account! I don't know the PIN number."*

In teens and young adults, victims may be attracted to a controlling individual when they feel inexperienced, insecure and overwhelmed by a change in their life situation. When parents are going through a divorce, a teen may attach to a controlling individual, feeling the controller may stabilise their life. Freshmen in college may be attracted to controlling individuals who promise to help them survive living away from home on a college campus.

In unhealthy relationships and definitely in Stockholm Syndrome there is a daily preoccupation with "trouble." Trouble is any individual, group, situation, comment, casual glance or cold meal that may produce a temper tantrum or verbal abuse from the controller or abuser. To survive, "trouble" is to be avoided at all costs. The victim must control situations that produce trouble. That may include avoiding family, friends, co-workers and anyone who may create "trouble" in the abusive relationship. The victim does not hate family and friends; they are only avoiding "trouble!" The victim also cleans the house, calms the children, scans the mail, avoids certain topics and anticipates every issue of the controller or abuse in an effort to avoid "trouble." In this situation, children who are noisy become "trouble." Loved ones and friends are sources of "trouble" for the victim who is attempting to avoid verbal or physical aggression.

Stockholm Syndrome in relationships is not uncommon. Law enforcement professionals are painfully aware of the situation - making a domestic dispute one of the high-risk calls during the work hours. Called by neighbours during a spousal abuse incident, the abuser is passive upon arrival of the police, only to find the abused spouse upset and threatening the officers if their abusive partner is arrested for domestic violence. In truth, the victim knows the abuser/controller will retaliate against him/her if they:

1. Encourage an arrest;
2. Offer statements about the abuse/fight that are deemed disloyal by the abuser;
3. Don't bail them out of jail as quickly as possible; and
4. Don't personally apologise for the situation - as though it was their fault.

Stockholm Syndrome produces an unhealthy bond with the controller and abuser. It is the reason many victims continue to support an abuser after the relationship is over. It's also the reason they continue to see "the good side" of an abusive individual and appear sympathetic to someone who has mentally and sometimes physically abused them.

[**Author's Note**]: Studies were made of the findings about nine hostage groups, battered women, concentration camp prisoners, cult members, prisoners of war, incest victims and physically and emotionally abused children. Bonding to the accuser occurred in all nine hostage groups. Abused women showed signs that they were grateful for any act of kindness shown to them. They denied the abuse, were hyper-vigilant to the abuser's needs, were suspicious of people trying to help them, found it difficult to leave the abuser and feared the abuser would come back to get them if they left. They denied the danger they were in and see their abuser as their only friend. This is the person who has given them life - the only person they have in their lives.

Therapists find great difficulty breaking down conditions that set up the syndrome. By explaining the syndrome to the women, it's sometimes possible to show them how they are guided by the abuser's thinking - not her own. These explanations help eliminate the self-blame that's prevalent in these women.

Giving up being abused is like giving up drugs. It's the hardest thing abused women who love their husbands have to do. This is because abuse is familiar to them and they're used to it. They don't even know abuse is happening to them any more - it's a way of life and the only way they know or think someone loves them.

Even abusers, who don't lay a hand on them, get crazy sometimes. Many would want to kill their wives, but don't have the courage to do so or want their victim to remain available for further abuse.

These batterers will never change - instead they'll get worse. The more resistant and strong their victims become, the worse they become. Some threaten their wives that they'll put them in mental institution, take away their children or kill them. Their victims live every day in fear.

They hit because they're mad at their wives or mad at someone else or at something that happened earlier that day. Many are unemployed, underemployed and unhappy with their lives. Everything that happens to him is her fault.

For children, their parent's fighting is familiar to them. They grow up with it and think that all families are the same. Alcohol plays a large part and often is a trigger for aggression, jealousy, envy and further aggression against their wives. They have a need to put wives and children down - to make themselves feel more important. They tell their wives that they're worthless, that they'd be nobody and penniless without them looking after them. The wives have recurring nightmares, spending their waking time in fear and feel defenceless against their husband's battering.

Conclusion

Most women are killed by men they know and more often than not, by boyfriends and husbands who abuse them and their children. Prison sentences need to fit the crime.

Chapter 4
SPOUSAL AND PARTNER ABUSE

Everyone's human and most people "fly off the handle" at one time or another with their spouses. A husband may wonder if he might batter his wife if he was mad enough. Because of their nearness to each other, couples may find that their disagreements turn out to be shouting matches where neither member seems to hear the other person's side of the dispute. This often results in louder and louder responses until one member storms off in a huff, while another may resort to pouting and withdrawal. This can result in a vicious circle of conflict.

It's unfortunate that couples wait until one or both are considering separation or divorce to obtain marriage counselling. When couples face the threat that the quality of their marriage is in jeopardy - they need help. If they'd been aware of a workable communication technique early in their marriage, the situation might not have reached the stage where their marriage was in trouble or resulted in domestic violence or spousal abuse.

About 30 people a year die in Queensland from domestic violence. In 2003, that included nine children. Betty Taylor, chairwoman of the Queensland Domestic and Family Violence Council is heading a campaign for the Queensland government to set up a task force to investigate fatal cases to try to prevent further deaths. She said, *"Domestic homicides are not random acts and often follow a history of abuse. Often many domestic homicides have predictive elements to them. Victims and/or perpetrators may have intersected with any number of agencies and systems prior to the homicide, with varying degrees of success."*

"The key to prevention of domestic homicide is gaining a better understanding of patterns, prior indicators and gaps in current responses."

Her group is lobbying to have a Domestic Violence Fatality Review Board (modelled on systems in other countries) set up in Queensland.

Much of the following information was compiled from two excellent workbooks on domestic violence. The first is the:"Domestic Violence -

An Information Book" booklet produced by the Domestic Violence Service Gold Coast (Queensland, Australia).

Domestic Violence Prevention Centre Gold Coast Inc.

Source: Department of Families, Housing and Community Affairs Fact Sheet 2 Women's Safety.

Most of the dangerous, abusive and violent behaviour that occurs in the privacy of people's homes is committed by men against women. The most recent information on violence in Australia comes from the Australian Bureau of Statistics, Personal Safety Survey (national survey of 16,400 adults in Australian aged 18 years and over) conducted in 2005. The first issue of this survey was conducted in 1996. The 2005 survey found:

- Just under half a million Australian women reported that they had experienced physical or sexual violence or sexual assault in the past 12 months.
- More than a million women had experienced physical or sexual assault by their male current or ex-partner since the age of 15 (some women may be counted twice if they experienced both physical and sexual assault).
- 37.8% of women who experienced physical assault in the 12 months before the survey said the perpetrator was a current or previous male partner and 34.4% said the perpetrator was a male family member or friend. Most incidences of physical assault against women in the 12 months prior to 2005 were committed in a home (64.1%).
- 33.3% of women had experienced physical violence since the age of 15.
- 19.1% of women had experienced sexual violence since the age of 15.
- 12.4% of women had been sexually abused before the age of 15, compared with 4.5% of men, between 1996 and 2005. There was an increase in the reporting of sexual assault to police from 14.9% to 18.9% between 1996 and 2005 and there was an increase in the reporting of physical violence to police from 18.5% to 36%.
- 64% of women who experienced physical assault and 81.1% of women who experienced sexual assault still did not report it to police. The proportion of women aged between 18 and 34 who reported experiencing physical violence has decreased but the

proportion of women who reported experiencing physical violence after 45 increased over the same period. The percentage of women who reported that their children had witnessed partner-related violence either from a current or ex-partner was lower than in 1996.
- Most of the violence against men is committed by other men. Of men who reported that they had experienced physical violence in the 12 months before the survey, 73.7% said that the perpetrator was a male.

Understanding Domestic Violence

Domestic violence is the use of any form of violence by one person to control another and is used to describe any abuse that occurs in intimate relationships. Although domestic violence against men does happen, the cases are few and very far between. Unfortunately the same cannot be said about their female counterparts.

In the majority of cases of domestic violence, the victims are women. The abuse may continue long after the relationship has ended. Generally women in domestic violence situations do not enter into a relationship believing that it will become violent. There are occasions when women may make long-term relationship commitments believing that marriage or a marriage-like commitment will put a stop to extreme jealousy and possessiveness. There are also occasions when women enter longer-term commitments out of fear.

For many women, physical and sexual violence does not begin until a year or so into a long-term relationship, often during pregnancy. The controlling and dominating behaviour prior to long-term commitment is often interpreted as jealousy and often considered a compliment to the woman or a sign of his love for her.

Within a relationship, disagreements and arguments do occur - this is normal and both partners should be able to put forward their different points of view or concerns and discuss them together. It is not normal for one partner to feel threatened, too frightened to argue back or too frightened to disagree or express his/her opinion. Research indicates that from 25 per cent to 31 per cent of homicides in Australia involve either spouses or sexual intimates.

Isolation

[The husband] cuts off the support systems that may help assaulted women break the cycle of violence. Husbands frequently attempt to control their partners' activities by isolating them. Often the abuser convinces his partner that family contacts and friendships interfere with the relationship and make already existing problems worse. He may try to cut family ties, further isolating the assaulted woman. In extreme cases, women are forbidden to leave the home at all and if they are permitted to leave, it must be in the company of the abuser. Feelings of loneliness and the despair common to isolated women can further immobilise them from breaking the cycle of violence.

Spousal Abuse [Author's Comments]

Almost half of all homicides are between spouses and most of the victims are women and come from a family where there was abuse.

Most men would argue that not all men are violent and that society shouldn't judge all men because of the actions of the men who are. Unfortunately, many of the men who condemn violence, abuse their wives and children because they don't consider their actions as being violent. Abuse that has its roots in childhood becomes part of a web of societal violence. Women are often fleeing mates who bring childhood abusive tactics into their adult relationships. They move from creating havoc in the classroom or schoolyard as children to being adults who create havoc in their homes. Regretfully, many child bullies mimic behaviours they have seen used by adults. These tactics seem to work - so they use them themselves.

The belief has been drummed into them, that men have the right to dominate women and thus, if they wish, they can abuse women. Fathers tell their sons, *"Don't hit your sister back - she's a girl."* Millions of these small boys hear such comments from their fathers who then turn around and beat their mothers because supper's late.

Spousal abuse has remained an unrecognised crime for centuries. Wife abuse involves a husband intimidating his wife, either by threat or by actual use of physical violence. His violence may be directed at her person or her property. The purpose of the assault is to control her behaviour. Sometimes the fear of violence is enough to establish that control. Underlying all abuse is a power imbalance between the victim and the offender.

Some commonly held beliefs prevent a complete understanding of the problem of wife assault. Many people believe wife assault occurs infrequently and rarely results in severe injury. It is also generally thought that wife assault occurs only in low-income families, to poorly educated women or only in certain cultures.

We now recognise wife assault as a major social problem that affects thousands of women every year and experts agree that more wife assault occurs than is reported.

When we hear of assaults between strangers, we have little trouble recognising one party as the victim and the other as the offender. Our attitudes towards these assaults are clear. The offender is guilty of committing a crime. Society supports our attitudes by making offenders responsible for their actions and punishes them in order to protect their victims. When we hear of assaults happening within relationships and families, however our attitudes are less clear.

Wife battering *is* a crime. Every citizen has the right to freedom from assault or from fear of assault. Wife assault involves the husband intimidating his wife, either by threat or by actual use of physical violence. The purpose of the assault is to control her behaviour. Sometimes the fear of violence is enough to establish control. Underlying all abuse is a power imbalance between the victim and the offender.

Abuse can be in the form of physical, sexual, psychological, destruction of property or pets and financial dependency. The longer the violence continues, the greater the chance is that the victim will experience all five forms of abuse. Survivors of wife assault, state their financial dependence on their partners was one of the main reasons for staying in the abusive relationships.

At one time in history, it was legal for a man to physically assault his wife as long as he did not use a stick any thicker than his thumb which is where the phrase "rule of thumb" comes from. Although this practice has been outlawed for over a hundred years, societal attitudes are very slow to change and many of our beliefs about relationships between men and women remain outdated. Some of our attitudes not only allow, but expect husbands to dominate and control their wives. In many relationships, wives may still be expected to obey and submit to their husband's demands. In relationships where physical violence is used as a method of control, our attitudes blur our ability to see wife assault as a crime. Instead wife assault is often viewed as a family problem, to be dealt with by the family. Where the victim recognises the assault as a crime, the guilt and humiliation she feels can sometimes stand in the way of her seeking help. As a result, thousands of women and their children continue to live in fear. Fortunately attitudes are changing.

The Women's Movement has been a driving force, increasing our awareness about wife assault. They have been a strong voice ensuring that women hear that equality in relationships is their right - not a privilege. Concerned individuals have worked hard to create shelters in our communities so that survivors of wife assault have safe places to go when they decide to reach out. Support groups for victims and offenders are established to provide a supportive network. Shelter services and other resources are available to people whether they choose to leave or remain in the abusive relationships.

The batterer, like a mugger, will deliberately choose a woman who seems least able to defend herself. Abused women don't go looking for thugs, but batterers can be very charming and can deceive them into believing that they're caring individuals. It's only after the woman has been exposed to his behaviour that a pattern begins to show.

Battering is not an occasional beating. It is a system of controlling a woman through terror, confusion, disabling and every imaginable brainwashing technique. Many battered women are prohibited from leaving their homes, forbidden to use birth control, prohibited from speaking with their friends and forbidden to work. They have no access to money. Women who started out strong and self-reliant have been battered into feeling weak, powerless and totally dependent.

Battered women are often deprived of sleep and become confused by their abuser's unpredictable actions and behaviour. This living in a constant state of terror is so debilitating that they lack the energy to think straight.

A US Surgeon General's report found that wife battery results in more injury to women than rape, auto accidents and muggings combined. In many cases, the first people who encounter these women are health care workers - doctors, nurses, paramedics and others who fail to identify or assist them beyond immediate treatment of their injuries. Although health care workers must report incidents of suspected child abuse, no such imperative exists in cases of wife beating. The widely held societal view is that the woman has probably brought the abuse on herself, is often shared by the victim. The severity of her injuries may cause her to seek medical help, but she's too humiliated or terrified to say how she got them. If the woman comes in with a sprained ankle and she says she fell - health care workers are likely to believe her.

Women who are abused were found to have poor health, suffer chronic pain and depression, attempt suicide, have addictions and experience problem pregnancies in greater numbers than women who are not abused.

Often the abusing husband is cheating on his wife. She will know that this is happening when he picks on her, finds fault with her, tells others she is crazy or stupid, works out more, takes more pride in his appearance, hides money, becomes distant and addicted to the internet and/or phone. [End of Author's Comments]

Drug and alcohol abuse

One of the most commonly held beliefs of the cause of domestic violence is alcohol or substance abuse. But the fact is that almost even numbers of sober and drunken men are violent. Where studies show that more drinkers are violent to their partners, the studies are not able to explain why many drunken men (80 per cent heavy and binge drinkers) did not abuse their wives.

In fact, men use alcohol or other addictive substances as a means to give themselves permission to be violent. If someone blames alcohol or drugs, they are avoiding taking responsibility for their actions. Many people enjoy drinking and some may even drink excessively and never get violent. Many people stop their drinking and still keep using violence and controlling behaviours. While the use of alcohol and drugs can often make the violence more serious, they do not cause it.

What about women who use violence?

Women's use of violence against their partners can take several forms:

- Self-defence - when women use violence to protect themselves.
- Retaliatory violence - when women hit back after experiencing a long history of abuse.
- Predominant aggressor violence - when women use violence as control.

There are a small number of women who use a pattern of abuse against their partners. There are also a small number of men who need protection from violence from either a female or male partner. Sometimes these men are ashamed or find it hard seeking help to be safe. However, most men report that they have been assaulted by other men, by a partner, adult son, father, brother or other.

Mutual Violence

Mutual abuse is not common. A 'fight' involving violence where both people are equal is rare. A pattern of violence that includes control and domination by one of the partners is more common. Where one person uses violence as a form of control, this person is known as the predominant aggressor.

Religion and Domestic Violence

"The Scriptures can sometimes be misused to condone the use of power and to keep women and children in unsafe situations; hence care offered by the church has often been destructive rather than liberating." (Ian George, Archbishop of Adelaide, 1995.)

When interpreting Bible or Koran texts, people may quote short passages out of context for their personal use. This can alter the meaning of the passage. Abusers may use their religion or religious affiliation as an excuse for their violence. Religion is no excuse for domestic violence. There is nothing to support the view that it is God's will for people to endure family violence. Some women may feel pressure from their faith or community to 'honour' their commitment to marriage and stay in an abusive relationship. They may think that to leave or get a divorce is against their religious beliefs.

Culture and Domestic Violence

It's important to maintain cultural traditions and beliefs, but this can be done without violence or abuse. Some abusive men claim that in their culture, women have a subordinate role and the use of violence is permitted to keep women in line. Some excuse the legal system of attempting to destroy their culture or that laws against family violence are racist.

[Author's Comments] Young Muslim girls (some living in Australia) are still being mutilated by castration when they're only six or eight years of age. From a Muslim male's point of view, it is done so that women will remain pure, but they rob their women of the pleasures of lovemaking.

Respecting a person's culture is important, but stopping that kind of violence is more important. Under the law the same standards of non-violent behaviour should apply to everybody regardless of their cultural background or religion. [End of Author's Comments]

Conclusion:

Abuse in homes is a universal, albeit complex phenomenon which has far reaching effects. Women who are abused were found to have poor health, suffer chronic pain and depression, attempt suicide, have addictions and experience problem pregnancies in greater numbers than women who are not abused.

Domestic violence has its roots deep in the past and is anchored in many cultural mindsets, whether one is talking about traditional cultures or in the developed world. Although some change in attitudes is taking place, much more needs to be done.

Abusers believe:

- They should be in control of their partners and/or children;
- Their needs and goals are more important than those of other family members;
- The person(s) they're abusing are inferior or unimportant;
- There is nothing wrong with controlling and punishing certain family members;
- That certain family members should behave in particular ways;
- That the abused persons have negative intentions and motives behind their behaviours.
- They have a right to use abusive behaviour;

They:

- Have inadequate or inappropriate knowledge and skills;
- Are unable or unwilling to stop their abusive behaviour;
- Have had experiences in their lives that have caused severe psychological harm to them.

Their victims believe:

- They have no way to escape or stop the abuse;
- They deserve the abuse;
- That the abuser has the right to control and/or punish them.

Physical, Sexual Violence Equals Power and Control; Vs: Non-Violence Equals Equality

The following information shows how things should be in an equal relationship. Neither partner needs to be the boss. Equality, trust and love must be paramount for there to be equality between men and women.

Economic Abuse:

- Keeps her from obtaining or keeping a job.
- Takes her money;
- Gives her an allowance or makes her ask for money;
- Gives her no knowledge of or access to family income.

Vs: Economic Partnership;

- Make money decisions together;
- Both partners benefit from financial arrangements.

Using coercion and threats;

Makes and/or carries out;

- Threats to do something to hurt her or the children;
- Threatening to leave her and/or the children;
- Deny her access to her children;
- Threats to commit suicide;
- Will report her to welfare;
- Make her drop charges;
- Make her do illegal things.

Vs: Negotiation and fairness;

- Conflicts are solved by seeking mutually satisfying resolutions;
- Both acceptable to change; Both are willing to compromise.

Emotional Abuse;

- Puts her down;
- Makes her feel bad about herself;
- Calls her names;
- Badgers her until she thinks she's crazy;
- Plays mind games;
- Humiliates her especially in public;
- Makes her feel guilty.

Vs: Mutual Respect;

- Listen to each other non-judgmentally;
- Are emotionally supportive and understanding;
- Value each others' opinions.

Intimidating;

- Makes her afraid by using looks, actions, gestures;
- Destroys things;
- Demolishes her possessions;
- Abuses pets;
- Shows weapons.

Vs: Non-Threatening Behaviour;

- Talk and act so she feels safe and comfortable;
- She can express herself and doing things without his permission.

Using male privilege;

- Treats her like a servant;
- Makes all the big decisions;
- Acts like the king of the castle;'
- He's the one who defines men's and women's roles.

Vs: Sharing responsibility;

- Mutually agree on a fair distribution of work;
- Make family decisions together.

Using children;

- To make her feel guilty;
- Uses the children to relay messages;
- Uses visits to harass her;
- Threatens to take the children away.

Vs: Responsible parenting;

- Shares parental responsibilities;
- Is a positive, non-violent role model for the children.

Minimising and denying abuse;

- Makes light of the abuse;
- Does not take her concerns about the abuse seriously;
- Denies that the abuse happened;
- Shifts responsibility for his abusive behaviour saying she caused it.

Vs: Honesty and Accountability;

- Accepts responsibility for self;
- Acknowledges past use of violence;
- Admits it when wrong;
- Communicates openly and truthfully.

Isolating;

- Controls what she does, who she sees or talks to, what she reads and where she goes;
- Limits her outside involvement; Uses jealousy to control actions.

Vs: Trust and support;

- Supports her life goals;
- Respects her right to her own feelings, friends, activities and opinions.

Safety

If you or someone you know is experiencing domestic violence, safety considerations must be a priority in any attempts to access support. Any threats need to be taken seriously. Safe homes and women's shelters ensure a safe environment for clients.

Dysfunctional homes

Men and women who have grown up in dysfunctional homes have tremendous barricades to overcome. These are families where we find child incest, where child and wife beating are the norm. As adults, these people don't really understand how "normal" families function. They have to guess and often revert to their memories of what to them was normal behaviour. Many people who have experienced family violence in their childhood accept violence as a method to resolve conflict. Therefore, family violence continues from generation to generation.

Factors related to bullying and victimisation:

Family factors related to bullying:

- Family has many stressors - financial, single parent, illness;
- Family has no social support;
- High level of parental conflict;
- Low monitoring of child's activities;
- Inconsistent or harsh punishment;
- Low levels of communication and/or intimacy.

Family factors related to victimisation:

- Overly protective parents;
- Lack of independence in family;
- Passive parents;
- Family pressures such as divorce, separation;
- Workaholic parents;
- Overwhelming sibling rivalry.

Why do men abuse?

Violence! It offers the man a quick solution to the disagreement. It helps him avoid talking about the real problem. And because men are physically stronger - they will win - so there won't be a problem the next time a similar problem arises.

Men get no instruction. The man has a wrong mentality about his role. If a man believes that it is part of his duty as the head of the family to control what his wife does, then he may feel it is okay to hurt her. He may not know any other way.

We like to think of masculinity as natural, but most of its manifestations are cultural and historical - rather than biological. They get the myth of masculinity being how James Bond acts by defeating the other guys, seducing the women and burning down the buildings. Still, all that is masculine is not bad. We just need to tear away the trappings and define masculinity in different terms. Masculinity on the one hand has meant strength and activity in protection of the family, but on the other hand it has also meant escape from domesticity and resistance to the control of women.

There are three dominant themes relating to the definition of masculinity that we grapple with. Men have a strong love/hate relationship with their own masculinity. It's a lifelong struggle. It takes priority over any real relationship in life. Many get stuck in the adolescent period. This struggle puts families and marriages at risk. What they do and how they do it can make them candidates for things like heart and circulatory disease - the number one cause of death. A look at mortality tables shows that men are more fragile in a survivorship sense than women. Some of this relates to lifestyle and how men deal with life.

The biggest advantage for women is that if they are having a problem coping, they seek help. Men don't. Emotionally, it's not part of their role. They aren't supposed to admit they have a problem. They're expected to be able to solve it. They believe they should be able to control problems and contain them, but there are some problems they just can't solve on their own. There lies the problem.

When the pressure becomes too much, they look for ways to relieve it through alcohol, drugs, overwork, hitting their wives/children or having affairs. When men are out of control with their masculinity, there are three kinds of behaviours they can portray that are harmful:

The Homoclyte.

This is the most insidious form of behaviour. Homoclytes are boring, rule-bound and afraid of their emotions. They have difficulty with intimate relationships. They live within a narrow range of emotions and they believe that set of emotions is right. That was the norm for men in the 1950s. More modern men may feel that any man who shows his feelings is out of control.

Men's value has been stripped down. A common misconception is that all they are expected to do is make money and die, leaving their families well off. Their value is determined by how much money they make.

The root of the problem is that they haven't been fathered properly. Fathers today are usually too busy playing at being masculine to take part in raising their sons. What a boy might see is his father out there fighting wars, working or chasing other women, proving he's not under anyone's control. There's been no strong model for them about what it is to be a man. So when a boy reaches adolescence, he begins to define masculinity as anything that isn't female. He will tend to exaggerate these differences because there is no role model. And society's answer to masculine behaviour is often *"A man's got to be what a man's got to be."* For some men, being masculine begins and ends with having a penis.

He feels Mom has the power to define whether or not he's a man and he begins to sense he has to escape her control. After all, she can remind him he's still a child. No matter how much he needs his mother, he doesn't want to be seen to need her. So he thinks that if he's dirty enough and loud enough he will feel masculine. He feels kinship only with other guys and if there are no grown men around, he will identify only with the other boys.

He turns to adolescent girls to have his masculinity affirmed. They don't know any more than he does. So much fear of female power comes from this time in a boy's life. It's a great set-up for infidelity, because in order to re-affirm his masculinity, he has to continue testing out his sexuality by seducing other women. Men act out the script they were given. They don't know who created the script, but they follow it.

When women pushed for independence, the shoe was put on the other foot. Men had to deal with things they don't have a script for. Part of the problem has been those telling them that they need to change - women. Yet men have been taught not to value females. Men have been blaming everything since Adam and Eve on women. What most of these men are trying to do is be masculine enough to get their father's approval. Most fathers' behaviour differs drastically from what has become the norm in society.

The Philanderer.

He has a desperate need to seduce women. And once he's done that - he discards them. The game is to score with women. A philanderer is basically very, very angry with women. He doesn't like them and that makes him dangerous. He's out to defeat them one by one. Unfortunately, women seem to be attracted to them.

The Competitor.

Life is a contest with the other guys. It all goes back to adolescence when he spent his time measuring his penis. This guy can make anything into a contest - how much money he makes, how many degrees his wife has, what his children have accomplished, his golf handicap and the kind of car he drives.

Conclusion:

It's not that men don't want to change. They just don't know how. If you ask a man to be more nurturing, he might really want to be. We're asking for a whole new masculine role. The question is - how can we make it happen? Perhaps the boys who have been raised in households with only a mother will be the ones helping make the shift to less gender identification of roles.

Relationship Abuse

Various types of abuse can occur within relationships. In most abusive relationships, more than one type of abuse occurs. The longer the violence is allowed to continue in the relationship, the greater the chance is of the victim experiencing all forms of abuse. Abuse includes controlling what she does, who she sees and talks to, where she goes, keeping her from making any friends, talking to her family or having any money. Or they prevent her from going to work, not allowing her to express her own feelings or thoughts, not allowing her any privacy, forcing her to go without food or water or not allowing cultural, religious or personal freedom. Their controlling behaviours are often linked to jealousy.

Emotional or psychological abuse - such as:

- Put-downs;
- Insults;

- Constant criticism;
- Blaming her for his abusive actions;
- Breaking down partner's belief system (cultural or religious);
- Making partner watch children or pets being abused and not allowing partner to intervene.

Fear is a key element in domestic violence and is often the most powerful way a perpetrator controls his victim. Fear can be created by looks, gestures, possession of weapons (even when they may not have been used) destruction of property, cruelty to pets - or any behaviour that can be used to intimidate and make the person feel powerless. [End of Author's Comments]

"Wife Assault - Hurts all of us"

The following information is excerpts from: *"Wife Assault - Hurts all of us"* a brochure prepared by Frances Cearns, Lenore Walker, Karen Neilsen and Edmonton Area Inter-Agency Committee on Wife Assault Services, Canada.

[Author's Comments] Thirty per cent of Canadian women who experience physical violence, report that their children have witnessed the violence. In every classroom, an average of four children saw a woman being abused within the past year. [End of Author's Comments]

Every woman has the right to carry on her life without fear of threats of assault from her spouse or partner. Threats of abuse are also legally considered assault whether they result in injury or not. A person commits an assault when:

- Without the consent of another person, he applies force intentionally to that other person, directly or indirectly;
- He attempts or threatens, by an act or gesture, to apply force to another person.
- If he has or causes that other person to believe upon reasonable grounds that he has the ability to do so;
- While openly wearing or carrying a weapon or an imitation thereof, he accosts or impedes another person.

Other forms of physical abuse may not seem as obvious as direct physical attack, but can be equally as dangerous. If she has been physically restrained from leaving or entering her home, left in a place where her safety was endangered or denied access to medical treatment when sick or injured, she has been physically abused. Permanent physical injuries are common among assaulted women and many women are killed by their husbands each year.

Psychological abuse is an attack on the victim's emotional well-being. There are many different forms of psychological abuse including name-calling, put-downs and being critical of her appearance and her abilities as a woman, wife, lover and mother. Abusing the woman by leading her to believe she is insane, stupid, 'a bad mother' or useless. Behaviour can include silence and withdrawal. The end result of constant verbal attacks is that the assaulted woman can lose the self-confidence necessary to maintain a positive self-image. Her self-esteem can become so low that she may feel incapable of making and following through with decisions necessary to break the cycle of violence. Assaulted women say that poor self-esteem is one of the main reasons they stay in abusive relationships.

Once an assaulted woman has been the victim of one episode of her partner's angry and violent behaviour, the fear of further assault is always present. It is the fear and intimidation felt by the woman that gives the abusive man power and control. He has behaved in a violent way, making his threats believable and uses this form of psychological abuse to control his partner. If she stays, he believes she has condoned his behaviour so it will continue. The bottom line is - once your partner becomes abusive, it's time to leave.

Isolation or Social abuse - such as:

- Denying the partner access to or the opportunity to keep friends, social contacts or outside interests;
- Jealousy;
- Making family contact difficult; and
- Physical/emotional abuse in public or in front of friends.

[End of Author's Comments]

Excessive Jealousy

Accusations of extra-marital affairs are common. Co-workers, male and female friends, family members and former partners can all be suspect. Even strangers who may pay some attention to the abused woman arouse his suspicions. No amount of reassurance can convince the abuser that his jealousy is unwarranted.

The assaulted woman is unable to show affection to anyone other than the abuser without fear of further abuse. Sometimes the abuser is jealous of the attention and time she spends with the children and demands her undivided attention.

[Author's Comments]

Intimidation - such as:

- Threats to hurt or kill children, pets, friends;
- Throwing things;
- Destruction of property;
- Controlling partner's talk;
- Making partner account for every minute, every action;
- Threats to hurt anyone who helps her;
- Threats to prove partner is an unfit mother;
- Threats of suicide; and
- Controlling with fear.

Intimidation includes harassing her at her workplace either by persistent phone calls or text messages, following her to and from work or loitering near work. It could also include smashing things, destroying her property, putting a fist through the wall, handling of guns or other weapons, intimidating body language (angry looks, raised voice), hostile questioning, reckless driving.

Physical abuse

Such as pushing, shoving, hitting, slapping, choking, hair pulling, punching, shaking, kicking, breaking bones, knifing, shooting or use of other weapons. [End of Author's Comments]

Destruction of property or pets

In some abusive relationships, abusers attempt to maintain control by destroying things that have great personal value to the assaulted woman. Gifts from other persons, objects that the abused woman may have created herself or items that may be impossible to replace are all targets of this type of abuse. Family pets can suffer at the hands of the abuser.

The object of this form of abuse is to intimidate the victim and force compliance. Destroying property and pets conveys the messages that, everything the victim values is worthless, that the abuser has the power to destroy things that have meaning for her and that the violence can always be re-directed to her.

[Author's Comments]

Sexual abuse - such as:

- Forced unwanted sex;
- Demanding that partner wear more (or less) provocative clothing;
- Forced sex with objects, friends, animals;
- Insisting that partner act out pornographic fantasies;
- Denial of partner's sexuality.

Forced sex (whether between unmarried or married couples) is rape. Sexual assault is an act of violence, power and control - it's not related to love. It can include many behaviours including forced sexual contact, rape, forcing her to perform sexual acts that cause pain or humiliation, forcing her to have sex with others, causing injury to sexual organs.

Marital rape is treated as a form of assault. Prior to legislation changes, husbands could not be charged with sexually assaulting their wives, even though sexual assault outside the marriage was considered a crime. It appeared that society considered consenting to marriage meant giving away all rights to protection from sexual practices that would be considered rape between strangers. Women in abusive relationships were forced to endure the consequences of this lack of protection.

Laws now assert that all persons have a right to control their own bodies and that sexual abuse within marriage is not a part of healthy relationships, but is a crime punishable by law.

Forced sexual contact during and following physical assaults, threats of abuse for failing to consent to sexual advances, being physically hurt during sex and being forced to commit degrading acts, are examples of sexual abuse.

Financial abuse - is one of the most common forms of abuse. Assaulted women who work full-time in the home are sometimes denied access to financial resources by their partners. The abusive man can maintain financial dependency and increase financial control by forbidding his partner to work outside the home. They make the victim financially dependent on them, demanding that their wives and children live on inadequate resources.

Abused women who work outside the home are often forced to hand over their paycheques to the abusive partner who makes decisions on how the money will be spent. Survivors of wife assault state that their financial dependence on their partners was one of the main reasons for staying in the abusive relationship.

The effects of abuse on women

Women who remain in abusive relationships after a pattern of violence has been established, experience a number of physical and emotional effects of the abuse. Physical effects range from cuts and bruises to death. Almost half of all homicides are between spouses and the majority of victims are women. The emotional and physical effects of wife assault become more severe the longer women remain in their abusive relationships.

[End of Author's Comments].

Self-esteem

Our self-esteem or self-concept is a measure of how we feel about ourselves. Low self-esteem creates feelings of self-doubt and worthlessness, eroding the self-confidence needed to make decisions and to solve problems. When our own feelings and judgement cannot be trusted, solving even small problems becomes difficult. In many cases, low self-esteem and poor self-concept may lead to depression. Depression is a medical condition that often requires medication or therapy to be effectively treated. Low self-esteem can also result in a disregard for personal appearance and health.

Feelings of helplessness

In abusive relationships, the abusive man maintains control of his partner's actions by physically, sexually and psychologically abusing her. If the assaulted woman tries to regain some control, the abuser may become more controlling. Her repeated unsuccessful attempts at stopping his violence reinforce her feelings of helplessness. As a result, the assaulted woman may give up trying to break the cycle of violence.

Self-blame and guilt

Looking after the emotional needs of the family has traditionally been the woman's job in our society. When the emotional well-being of the family is suffering, as it does in abusive relationships, the woman blames herself, believing she has failed in her role as emotional caretaker. Some assaulted women have hidden their abusive relationships for years because of the guilt and shame they have felt. The abusive partner reinforces the self-blame and guilt the victim feels by blaming her for the abuse. The end result of this self-blame and guilt is that the assaulted woman may come to falsely believe that since she has failed as emotional caretaker, she causes and deserves the abuse.

Denying and Minimising

Denying and minimising abuse are two ways of coping with his violence although they are ineffective. They increase the danger already present by encouraging the victim to disregard signals that can warn her of further assaults.

Abused women frequently deny being victims of wife assault and that a pattern of wife assault has been established. A false sense of responsibility for the violence and embarrassment prevent her from telling others about it. Other excuses can be made to explain away the violence and to renew hope for the relationship.

Minimising abuse downplays its seriousness. Often women avoid accepting the reality that they are being abused, by comparing themselves to others who have endured more extreme acts of physical and psychological abuse. Their own situations then seem much less serious and dangerous.

Drug and alcohol abuse

Victims of wife assault suffer from stress and tension. Many abused women turn to drugs and alcohol to avoid confronting their abusive situations. Continued use of these substances leads to dependency for many women. Substance abuse adds to the assaulted woman's problems. The abused woman who tries to deal effectively with her substance dependence and her violent situation at the same time is easily over-whelmed.

Alcohol and illegal drugs are obvious examples of abused substances, but abuse of prescription drugs accounts for much of the substance abuse among victims of wife assault. Sleeping pills, painkillers and tranquillisers are some of the more commonly abused prescription drugs.

Conforming to abusive behaviour

In abusive relationships where the cycle of violence continues without intervention, physical and psychological abuse can become the assaulted woman's methods of problem solving. The combined effect of low self-esteem, feelings of helplessness and despair and the false belief that she has caused and deserved the abuse creates a sense of desperation. This can lead the abused women to the use of violence in order to regain some measure of control over her life. Very few women who become abusive reach out for help to break the cycle of violence when violence has been accepted as normal behaviour in their relationships. Intervention is aimed at protecting children of these relationships as they often become targets of physical and psychological abuse and pass it on to the next generation when they marry.

Counselling

Talking to someone about domestic violence is often difficult. Seeking counselling does not mean there is something wrong with a person, but more that something wrong has happened to them. Counsellors assist women to make safe choices for themselves and their children. They can provide information on support and services available and assist with safety planning. They are not there to take over or force women into decisions. They can help women deal with a range of feelings and fears associated with abuse. Crisis appointments are available for women with immediate and urgent physical and emotional safety concerns.

Clients have the right to confidentiality with the following exceptions:

- If information is disclosed concerning a child who is 'at risk;'
- If the client is at risk of harming themselves or others; or
- If a court subpoenas a court file.

Those suffering from domestic violence have a right to:

- Live without fear of violence;
- Have their safety concerns heard and taken seriously;
- Have access to services which provide a safe environment;

- Have their immediate safety needs addressed;
- Be treated with respect, dignity and sensitivity;
- Have their experiences of violence heard and believed;
- Be treated as an individual with specific needs;
- Have access to services which respond to their individual and specific needs;
- Receive accurate information provided in a timely manner;
- Make their own decisions;
- Know the service limitations on confidentiality;
- Access clear pathways through the various systems;
- Counselling, advocacy and opportunities for healing;
- Have access to professionally qualified and trained counsellors; and
- Provide feedback on services received.

Learning Violent Behaviour

When children grow up watching violence used as a method of solving problems and managing stress, they learn that violence has a place in their families and that violence is normal behaviour. If a mother remains in the abusive relationship after being assaulted and the father is not made accountable for his violent behaviour, children learn that there are few consequences for violent behaviour. Children from violent homes, even those who grow up to reject their parents' abusive lifestyle, are more likely to find themselves turning to violence as adults than children from non-violent homes. Over three-quarters of all mothers in shelters had been abused as children and many gave this as a reason for staying in the abusive relationship.

(Courtesy of Karen Nielsen, M.Ed, RSW, The Family Centre, Edmonton, Alberta)

Children who witness wife abuse

Children need not be physically or sexually assaulted to be hurt by wife assault. Those who witness violence in the home are also victims.

How children are affected by witnessing wife abuse depends on a number of factors such as their age when the abuse began, how Mom coped and what help and support the child and Mom received.

Infants:

During the crisis, the baby's routine can be interrupted, causing the baby stress. An abused mom may have difficulty coping with a baby's demands at this time. The baby may not form a healthy emotional connection with either parent and so may grow up with many severe psychological problems. The baby may tend to sleep poorly, scream excessively, have poor health or fail to thrive.

Pre-School and school-aged children

Children deal with the stress of witnessing wife abuse in two ways: they hold it inside (internalise) or they express it (externalise). A child may learn the role of either the abuser or the victim and act out these roles. They may, for example, use aggression to solve problems with others at school. Children as young as 2 years old have been observed to act out adult violence they have witnessed. Boys are more likely to be aggressive, while girls more frequently act out their stress and anxiety by having health complaints (headaches, stomach aches) and by passive, dependent behaviour (they get "picked on" and don't stand up for themselves assertively).

Children who witness wife abuse often have low self-esteem, feel anxious and fearful much of the time, misunderstand the actions of others, become withdrawn and confused and have difficulty getting along with other children. Preschoolers tend to yell more, be more irritable, stutter, shake, rock, have nightmares and other sleep disturbances. Children under 10 years tend to blame themselves and believe that they are the cause of the violence. In general, young children who witness wife abuse are less able to solve personal problems in assertive and healthy ways.

Adolescents

Boys may become abusive in their own dating relationships. Girls may accept abuse from boys as a normal part of having a boyfriend. May act out in aggressive or delinquent ways: running away, assaulting their mother and younger family members, attempting suicide, drug and alcohol abuse, poor school performance. Teens frequently assume parenting roles in their family and assume the role of protector. They become "too old, too fast" and don't get to enjoy their teen years. Children 11 years and up don't usually blame themselves for the violence, but they don't necessarily assign responsibility to the abuser either. They may well excuse him and may side with him because he has the power in the family. They may feel angry with Mom for not protecting herself.

When parents separate or Dad stops his violence

When the children begin to feel safe, they will often talk about the abuse or draw pictures of it. This is their way of dealing with it and making sense of it. This is normal and healthy behaviour and should not be stifled.

If the parents separate, the children often have mixed feelings. Even though they are relieved to be safe, they may also feel sad and miss their father. It is important that children are told that it is all right for them to have conflicting feelings.

They may look to Mom for extra attention and reassurance. This can be a very difficult time for Mom because she has so many of her own problems to deal with. It can be very helpful if she joins a women's support group so she can get the help she needs. She and the children may be helped by having counselling together and the children may benefit a great deal in a children's group.

Conclusion:

There are many forms of abuse, both physical and emotional. Some of them are quite easily identifiable as abuse. Others, like intimidation or financial abuse are more subtle. However, all of them should not form a part of healthy relationships between spouses. Where such abuse occurs, homes quickly become dysfunctional. This has terrible effects on women and children in such a home. Ultimately, it sets up a cycle of abuse.

[Author's Comments]

Cycle of abuse

Domestic violence involves a cycle of abuse:
1. Husband/partner beats;
2. Husband/partner apologises - courts wife, gives gifts;
3. Honeymoon stage - wife may feel guilty that she made him feel so bad that he had to hit her. She feels the need to be punished for doing this; and
4. Repeat of the above.

As the cycle unfolds, the woman's endorphins are charged. This can affect her as if she was on drugs and when that cycle ends she has an emotional downer. The excitement associated with the danger has gone. This can be addictive.

She must replace those negative "highs" with positive feelings related to the challenge of changing her environment and using her abilities to find a better way of life. Unfortunately, most women who came from battered homes don't know that life should be any different. Society must help them learn that there is a better way of life awaiting them. Television, newspapers and community services are slowly highlighting that domestic abuse is unacceptable. [End of Author's Comments]

Cycle of Violence

One way of understanding abusive relationships is to see the violence as part of a larger cycle. Lenore Walker who has written ***The Battered Woma***) offers a theory about this cycle of violence. Rather than explaining what causes wife assault, the theory points to some reasons why women stay in abusive relationships.

Walker's cycle has three distinct phases: tension building, battering and remorse / contrite. One follows the next with no set length for any phase.

The tension-building phase

Positive as well as negative experiences in daily living create stress. Stress and tension do not cause wife assault, but they can act to trigger abuse. Unresolved tension can cause anger and frustration to build and psychological abuse may become the outlet in the tension-building phase. Afraid of her partner's mounting anger, the abused woman may appear passive and accepting of the psychological abuse as a way of calming his anger.

Although the abused woman may appear passive and accepting on the surface, inside her, anger and frustration are building. Afraid that disclosing her feelings will cause further abuse, she becomes withdrawn. The more she withdraws, the more controlling her partner can become. As tension builds, the psychological abuse becomes more frequent and intense. In many abusive relationships, this abuse can occur daily until the tension becomes unbearable.

The abused woman may try to control outside influences to ease tension. Common examples of this are making excuses for his behaviour and avoiding contact with family and friends. This increases isolation and separates her from those who may want to help her.

The battering phase

This is the phase where physical abuse takes over from psychological abuse. The battering phase may be triggered by the explosion of the abusive man's anger or by an external event. There is no way to determine how severe the assault will be because anger and frustration have reached the point where they seem uncontrollable. There is usually no way an abused women can stop the assault. The abusive man decides when the attack will stop. If she tries to fight back, she faces the risk of greater injury.

The battering phase is the shortest phase in the cycle of violence. It often lasts only a number of hours although some victims report battering incidents continue over a number of days.

Fear of further assault frequently stops the abused woman from seeking medical attention for her injuries. In many cases abusive partners knowing that their actions are criminal, wrong and may have consequences, prevent their victims from seeking medical help. If she does seek medical help, she may deny being abused.

Another reason why abused women do not reach out for help during the battering phase is that many suffer an emotional collapse within one or two days of the assault. Reactions, very similar to those of disaster victims occur. Feelings of shame, hopelessness and helplessness are common and abused women tend to remain isolated for a number of days after the assault.

Remorse and contrite phase (The honeymoon phase)

The tension that has built up is released in the battering phase. The honeymoon phase follows directly after the battering incident. Apologies for violence from the abuser, promises it will never happen again and his begging for forgiveness are all common in this phase. The abusive man may say he is sincerely sorry for the assault and both partners then may believe he will not be violent to her again.

Shelter staff usually see victims of wife assault as the battering phase is ending and the honeymoon phase is beginning. Women who have recently experienced severe physical and emotional traumas may be more motivated to consider making major changes in their lives.

Once the honeymoon phase is underway and if she has contact with the abuser, the victims' attitudes towards her situation often change. The abuser frequently reminds his partner how much he needs her. He reminds her that she will be breaking up the family if she goes or stays away. He attempts to convince her that even though he was wrong to beat her up, if he goes to jail, it will be her fault. He may threaten to harm her, the children, himself and others if she threatens to leave him.

Even though the abusive man may heap apologies, love and promises on his victim during this phase, she still suffers guilt and responsibility should he try to kill himself over what has happened (especially if he has tried suicide before) shame over not being able to keep her family together and; fear of spending her future alone. These factors work against the victim in the honeymoon phase and may make this the most difficult time for her to break the cycle of violence.

If the abused woman chooses to believe that the loving behaviour she witnesses during the honeymoon phase is the true indicator of what her partner is like, she will probably return to the relationship. Once she returns, the honeymoon phase may last for a number of days, weeks or months before the loving behaviour gives way to renewed psychological abuse and the cycle of violence continues.

Women who have remained with the abuser have reported that the period between assaults becomes shorter. In some cases the honeymoon phase disappears completely. With each new battering phase, violence becomes more severe and injuries more serious. Continued battering lowers her self-esteem and increases her isolation, making it more difficult to break the cycle of violence. It is important to note that minimising the abuse and especially denial of abuse and its effects, keep the cycle of violence going.

The abusive man

Traditional attitudes have supported the domination of women by men in all areas of their society including the family. The old "rule of thumb" law illustrates how totally men have been allowed and encouraged to control their partners. The law has changed, but society's belief in male dominance remains very strong.

Failure to arrest, charge and prosecute offenders further encourages men to use force to control their partner's behaviour. Legal and social responses have been inadequate in terms of enforcing consequences for wife assaulters. There has been a tendency for police, judges and lawyers to treat wife assaulters more leniently than those who assault people rather than their partners. Few programs and services exist to help the abusive man change his behaviour. Voluntary participation, rather than court ordered participation, leaves the onus on the often-unmotivated offender to attend.

The Need to control within intimate relationships

Assaultive men seem to share common beliefs about how they should behave within their relationships. Abusive men work at gaining and maintaining control in their relationships. Physical, sexual and psychological abuse, threats of abuse and financial dependency are all methods of enforcing control over victims. The abusive man attempts to make her comply with his wishes. If she challenges this or refuses, more abuse may result. Ironically, his need to control comes from his feeling that she controls him.

Although he may feel guilt and remorse as a result of his abuse of her, he continues to abuse her in an attempt to get her to stop doing those things that he believes makes him hit her.

Taking Responsibility

Attempts to control her may become extensive, strict and violent. Women are sometimes forced to neglect the physical and emotional needs of the children or to quit jobs or miss days off work for no reason. Often a double standard of acceptable behaviour develops - one set of rules for the offender and one for the victim. An example of the double standard i.e.: he insists that she stay home, however he is free to go out; he denies her access to financial resources while he has complete access.

Denial and blaming

Denying and downplaying the seriousness of wife assault is a way of avoiding the problem and its consequences. If an offender denies responsibility, he sees no need to change his behaviour. Denial is also used as an attempt to cope with the offender's own guilt and anxiety after he has abused his partner. The majority of men who assault their partners do not hold themselves responsible for their actions. Offenders frequently blame their partners for provoking them or causing abuse. Excuses such as, *"Look what you made me do."* Or, *"If you hadn't done that, none of this would have happened."* Or, *"She made me hit her"* or, *"She wouldn't be quiet"* or, *"She nagged me until I had to do something,"* are common. Other external factors - such as job pressures, friend or family disputes, even the weather, are used by assaultive men to explain their abuse. Once an external factor is blamed, the offender can justify that he was driven to use violence and need not accept responsibility for his actions. In reality, he is responsible for his behaviour - as she is responsible for hers.

Dependency and lack of empathy

Abusive men depend on their partners to meet most of their emotional needs. Many abused women compare their partner's emotional dependency to having another child to take care of. Perhaps because of jealousy or unmet needs, men may become violent when their wives are pregnant or soon after they give birth. Because babies are totally dependent, mothers have less time to meet their partners' needs.

Abusive men fear losing their partners and see outside influences as capable of pulling them away. Feeling threatened, men often attempt to reduce her contact with others, by forbidding her to talk or dance with others or to let her attend social gatherings by herself. When women pull away from the smothering feeling that jealousy and possessiveness create, the abusive man feels he's losing his partner and clings more tightly.

Empathy means being able to step into another person's place and experience a situation from their point of view. Abusive men find this difficult to do. They expect themselves to meet all of their partners' needs and that wives should require nothing more to satisfy them. Abusive men also expect their relationships with their wives and partners to take the place of relationships with friends. They find it difficult to take responsibility for their own happiness.

The abusive man's lack of empathy prevents him from fully understanding the impact his violent behaviour has on her sense of safety, dignity, well being and worthiness.

Change in the abusive man's behaviour

Abusive men require professional help to change attitudes. There are no guarantees that counselling will help him change, as counselling is only a guide for people who want to change themselves.

Men attend counselling for a variety of reasons. However few abusers will attend voluntarily. Some men do well in counselling and others will drop out shortly after they have begun. Choosing to stop his violence and take responsibility for his behaviour are the first important steps in counselling. Choosing to change lifestyle, attitudes and behaviours are hard work and take time. Two or three counselling sessions are unlikely to result in any improvement.

Although partners can provide moral support during counselling, one partner cannot make the other partner change. The offender must take responsibility for changing himself and make a serious commitment to follow through with changes. Offenders who attend counselling in an attempt to get their wives to stay in or to return to the relationship, often drop out early or fail to make progress in counselling. So counselling should be obtained while the couple is separated.

Most abusive men otherwise lead law abiding lives. They may enjoy jobs or careers and hold positions of respect in their communities. Some abusive men also assault other non-family members. There are differences in how these two groups of offenders perceive the consequences of their violence. Arrest and conviction for assault may be much more of a deterrent for the wife assaulter whose violent behaviour is hidden from public view than for the offender who leads a generally violent lifestyle. Those men who assault only their partners may be more likely to succeed in treatment programs.

One factor that is common to all abusive men is that they choose to use violence to control their partners. Wife assault is not accidental violence as offenders make a conscious decision to use force and threats of force.

[Author's Comments]

Transference of Anger:

Unable to face what they're really angry about, they shift it to another cause. For example something goes wrong at a party. The man says nothing, but later blames his spouse for something minor she did.

Long battles

These often don't concern what the person's really angry about. They occur because they've shifted their goal from sharing, to feelings of hurting the other person. They forget where they want to go. Their anger takes over and they can't stop themselves.

Explaining the behaviour of abused women

Why do abused women remain in battered relationships? Battered wives stay in relationships for many reasons. Many hope to change a man they love. At other times, he may be genuinely penitent, loving and generous. Women may feel they're to blame and try to change. They don't want to admit the marriage is a failure. They feel ashamed and isolated, but most of all - women stay because they have nowhere to go. They've been told so often, *"I know what's best for you"* and, *"I know what you want (or need)"* that they believe their abusers. The reality is that no one knows what is best for another adult.

These women feel trapped. They don't stay in abusive situations because they like it, but because their husbands have been successful in making them believe:

- That things will get better;
- They will be beaten more severely if they take action;
- His threats that he will kill or harm them, their children and other family members;
- They're dependent on their partner for shelter, food and other necessities so they could never survive on their own;
- Isolated because no one understands or believes them;
- That children need two parents and don't want to raise them alone;
- That they should keep the family together and live up to their religious commitment to remain with their partner;
- They won't be able to take care of themselves and their children alone;
- Their partners if he threaten to commit suicide if they leave;
- That no one else will love them - that no other man would want them;
- Their family and friends will reject them;
- They should feel ashamed, embarrassed and humiliated;
- They don't want anyone to know what is happening;

- Others will believe that they are stupid for staying as long as they already have;
- That they will be deported or that their children will be taken out of the country;
- They could never get a job (their husbands have repeatedly told them they couldn't);
- They deserve the abuse because they're so stupid, ugly ..."

It's believed that many of these women exhibit a behaviour seen in classic hostage situations. By better understanding this behaviour, therapists hope to develop more effective techniques to help women help themselves. [End of Author's Comments].

Conclusion:

Domestic Violence is a highly complex phenomenon. We need to fully understand its causes, forms and effects in order to be able to help others and even ourselves. Furthermore, dealing with domestic violence requires action from individuals, families and society at large. Lastly, attending counselling is no guarantee that an abuser will change his ways.

Chapter 5
CASE STUDIES - DOMESTIC VIOLENCE

Australian police deal with a domestic violence matter every two minutes by Clare Blumer: [Updated Fri 5 Jun 2015, 5:57am]

Australian police deal with an estimated 657 domestic violence matters on average every day of the year. That's one every two minutes.

Those figures are based on data provided by police services around the country about how often their officers work on domestic violence cases.

Overall, the count is 239,846 per year around the country.

There is no standard definition of domestic and family violence across all jurisdictions in Australia and no standard way for counting the number of police call-outs to situations related to domestic violence.

The details of the data being captured varies across jurisdictions and can include:

- attendance at suspected domestic and family violence incidents;
- domestic and family violence assaults (encompassing threats and physical violence); and
- domestic and family violence court orders made by the police;
- associated agencies reporting domestic and family violence to the police.

The breakdown of data is as follows.

	Date range	Description	by hour	by day	by week	by year
Victoria	2014	Family incidents	8	187	1,307	68,134*
Queensland	2013-14	Domestic and family violence	8	181	1,266	66,016*

	Date range	Description	by hour	by day	by week	by year
NSW	2014	Domestic violence related incidents occurrences	7	159	1,115	58,140*
Tasmania	2013-14	Family violence arguments and incidents	0	11	78	4,071*
WA	2013-14	Domestic assaults	2	41	289	15,095*
ACT	2013-14	Police attending domestic violence incidents	0	9	63	3,309*
NT	2014	Domestic violence assaults	0	12	81	4,224*
SA	2015	Domestic-related taskings	2	57	400*	20,857
Australia			**27**	**657**	**4,600**	**239,846**

Figure provided by state and territory police. Other numbers are calculated based on this figure and rounded to nearest whole number.

Some people think it must be easy for a woman to leave a relationship where domestic violence is happening - a woman can just get up and go. The truth is it is much harder to leave an abusive relationship than a non-abusive one. Many women do leave or try to leave, but find it a difficult and lonely process. Leaving her abuser does not necessarily mean that she will be safer.

For some women, especially immigrant women or women from indigenous backgrounds, leaving is not an easy option because they may be excluded from their support networks, the very group that gives them their standing with their relatives and their community.

Here are some quotes from women who have experienced domestic violence in their relationships and have expressed how they felt:

"For years he had me believing it was my fault. He made me think I was stupid and ugly and I deserved what I got. I was scared. He told me that I could never manage without him and no-one would ever want me or give me a job."

"I loved him - I still do really. He put me in hospital twice, but I just melted when I saw him crying after he beat me. I thought hitting me showed he cared. I believed him when he said he would change."

"He turned everyone against me. I had no friends, no social life and no support. He got the children to keep track of my movements and tell him what I'd been doing and whom I'd talked to. I knew he'd never let me go."

"My mother, his mother, our counsellor and our minister all told me I should stay. They said he was trying to change and I needed to support him. I waited through six years of hell."

Case Study – Car Ramming and Bashing

On 8 September, 2015, 24 year-old Tara Brown was chased in her car and rammed off the road by Lionel Patea, 24, the father of Ms Brown's child and a former Bandidos bikie gang member.

Tara Brown had sought help from police on domestic-violence-related issues days before she was allegedly beaten with a metal plate while trapped in her upturned car. She had been on life support after the attack on Tuesday but died about 9:00 pm on Wednesday night at the Gold Coast University Hospital.

Lionel Patea was charged with attempted murder at a hospital bedside hearing on Tuesday, where he was recovering from what are believed to self-inflicted stab wounds to the neck and chest.

In a statement, the Queensland Police Service said those charges would be upgraded to murder.

Case Study – *Woman killed at McDonalds*

On 11 September, 2015, a mother of four, Karina Lock, 49, was shot dead in front of horrified diners at a Helensvale McDonald's restaurant. She had left her old life - and her former partner 57-year-old Stephen Lock - behind in Maryborough last month to make a fresh start with her teenage daughter on the Gold Coast.

It's understood that she agreed to meet him that morning at McDonald's just after 9:00 am because it was a public place. This prearranged meeting ended in an argument. He shot her in the back, and she ran into the restaurant. Stephen followed about 30 seconds later, put his arm around her and shot her in the head. She died on the floor of the restaurant as diners and employees cowered in terror.

Then he stood over her and turned the gun in himself. Mr. Lock was taken to Gold Coast Hospital, placed on life support but died that afternoon.

Case Study - *Single Mum*

I grew up in a slum and had a white-trash background. When I was four, I was sexually molested by a family member and finally found the courage to make him stop when I was twelve. That experience left me emotionally scarred.

I eloped when I was fifteen and had a baby. My husband was an alcoholic and extremely abusive. His constant put-downs reinforced the feelings of low self-esteem that kept me trapped. I believed I was too dumb to do better. When he sexually molested a twelve-year-old neighbour girl, I had him arrested then left.

At nineteen, I was an uneducated, single mother. Earning opportunities were scarce, but somehow I managed to scratch out an existence. Two years later, I took a hard look at my future. I had two choices - stay stuck in the rut of self-pity forever or get an education and make something of my life.

I got my high school diploma by taking night classes and a university counsellor helped me apply for a government grant for my first year of college. I earned scholarships for the years that followed. Then I went to university during the day and worked as a waitress in the evenings.

Six years later, I graduated with a degree in business administration and went on to become a certified public accountant. Was I proud of myself? You'd better believe it. I now have the self-confidence that comes with independence and know I will never feel desperate again. The education I so doggedly pursued has given me tremendous freedom and I know that the sky is the limit.

Being born poor doesn't mean you have to stay that way for the rest of your life.

Case Study - Police Officer

Until she shot and killed her husband after years of enduring his physical abuse, Mytokia Friend was a Baltimore policewoman by day - a battered wife by night. Friend never consulted a doctor for treatment of the wounds inflicted by her husband, who was a Baltimore corrections officer. She was just too ashamed. But even if she had, she might well have received little or no help beyond treatment of her immediate injuries. One of the reasons women get to the point where they kill is that they don't receive any assistance from others.

Physicians fail to detect the true problem, because many women are reluctant to report they are being beaten. Battered women don't report abuse for a variety of reasons. They face the very legitimate fear that their partners will carry out their threats of retaliatory violence, not only against them - but against the children and other family members.

Friend is one of eight women whose sentences for killing their abusive spouses were commuted in 1991.

Case Study - Russ

I remained with my husband, Russ for thirteen years. During that time, I didn't realise that Russ was an abusive husband - just that I was terribly depressed and unhappy.

One incident demonstrated Russ's approval of violent spousal behaviour. We'd gone to his favourite tavern. Russ's friend Gary, who had left his wife Barbara at home with their children, became so drunk, that we drove him home. He insisted that we come in and have a cup of coffee. He went into the bedroom and woke Barbara and ordered her to make coffee for us. He became abusive to her and even though she was five months pregnant - shoved her against the wall. I looked at Russ to see what he was going to do about the situation, but he did nothing. I stepped in front of Barbara and threatened Gary that I would call the police and charge him with assaulting his wife if he touched her again. It took a long time before I spoke to either Gary or Russ again.

It was later that I examined my marriage and found that Russ had done many of the things that abusive people do:

Isolation - He wanted me at home with our children so I was not allowed to work. Slowly, but surely my friends drifted away, because he would not socialise with them. He had few friends of his own, so I was very lonely and had full responsibility for the children. He worked shift work (mainly four to twelve shift) and weekends and when he was home he ignored the children and me. Instead, he went to his workshop in the basement to putter with his tools.

Financial - I had to account for every penny I spent - had no income of my own. When I did take a part-time job to earn money one Christmas, he made it clear that I was still responsible for the complete care of the home and the children.

Sexual - He would often make lewd advances to me in the presence of our children - running his hands over my breasts or surprising me when I was cooking by coming up behind me and putting his hands around me to grab me by the crotch. He knew this annoyed me, but became angry when I shunned his advances. He didn't seem to understand that he repelled me with these actions. He also had bad body odour. Although he worked at a labouring job, he would only have one or two baths per week. He insisted on having baths instead of showers, because he expected me to stop whatever I was doing to scrub his back. I often sent in one of our boys to do this chore. I guess he thought this action would turn me on sexually - but it just turned me off.

Whether I liked it or not, he expected to have sex every night. This would normally take five minutes or less. There was little or no foreplay and he never allowed me time to get ready. Besides - he smelled.

A neighbour (twice my age) was forever making sexual advances towards me when we were out socially - sitting beside me and running his hand up and down my thigh. I kept moving away from him. Russ was aware of this, but just smiled and did nothing. When I was in the yard alone with the children, I often caught the neighbour spying on me from his upstairs window. When this man made a financial offer to Russ to spend the night with me, Russ seemed to be pleased at the man's comments - instead of defending me against such lewd suggestions.

Emotional/psychological - When I asked for a divorce, Russ refused to leave the home. I moved into my sons' room and put their beds in the family room. One day when I was getting an outfit out of the master bedroom, I noticed a rifle leaning against the wall. Russ knew I was deathly afraid of rifles. I checked and saw that it was fully loaded. I removed the bullets and then wondered what I should do with them. I buried them deeply in the garden. I had to repeat this again the next week. When the rifle was loaded a third time, my mind snapped.

I had thoughts of pointing the rifle at Russ and pulling the trigger. I was so appalled and shocked by my violent thoughts, that I unloaded it again, buried the bullets as usual, then went down to the basement, picked up a sledge hammer and smashed the rifle into a hundred pieces. Then I smashed the vacuum cleaner that Russ had promised to fix three months ago, along with all the other items he had promised to fix. When my rage was over, I left the mess for him to see.

Our social life was almost non-existent, but when we did go out, it was to his choice of tavern that had a live band. Most of the people got up to dance. Russ knew that I loved to dance, but I was forced to sit and watch everybody else dancing because he refused to do so. If I danced with other men, he would be calm at the tavern, but took out his rage on me later by forcing me to have very rough sex.

After I asked him for a divorce, he would come home from work at midnight and turn the stereo on full blast waking the entire family. One night when he was drunk, he came into my bedroom and tried to force himself on me (he's 6'4" tall and 230 pounds). My eleven-year-old son, who was sleeping in the basement, heard my struggles and came upstairs with a golf club - ready to hit his father. I saw him and yelled, *"No."* Russ saw him and I said to him, *"Look at what you're doing to your children. You should be ashamed of yourself!"* He got up, staggered past our son and slammed the bedroom door so hard the entire neighbourhood must have heard it. Russ didn't try to rape me again. The next week, I moved out of our family home.

There's always a final straw that breaks a relationship. I'd had two pregnancies that ended when my water broke when I was seven months pregnant. Although we had taken precautions, I found myself pregnant again and my doctor cautioned me that I must obtain help during my last trimester. When the time came to get help, Russ's answer was *"We can't afford it. We'll just have to manage somehow. I'll do what I can and the boys can help out more. There's no reason why they can't do the laundry and wash floors!"* This made sense, but who would run around after our two-year-old daughter, provide meals, do the shopping and the thousands of other duties I faced single-handedly? I knew Russ wouldn't help much himself and rather than start another argument, decided to make the best of things. I tried to rest more, but found it almost impossible.

When I had just entered my seventh month of pregnancy, my water broke about 3:30 p.m. just after Russ had left for work. A neighbour drove me to the hospital and called Russ at work. I'd been in the hospital for two hours when I had my first labour pain - but it was far stronger than what I normally felt at the onset of labour. I also felt icy cold, was perspiring heavily and began to shiver violently. The nurse applied several heated flannelette sheets, I stopped shivering and my labour pains stopped but I felt very weak. Thirty minutes later I noticed that something was dreadfully wrong. My active baby was suddenly very still. Since my fever began, I hadn't felt much movement. At 6:00 my doctor confirmed that the baby was in trouble and said he would call a specialist to do an immediate caesarean.

It took two more hours before the specialist arrived and still no sign of Russ. The specialist checked the baby's heartbeat, shook his head and said the simple, distressing words, *"It's too late - the baby's dead. We won't do the caesarean. Instead we'll wait until you go into labour naturally. Because you have a 105° temperature, the longer we can hold off delivery the better."*

I asked them to call Russ again. When the two doctors left the room, I heard what they said as they stood outside my room, *"She may not make it through the night unless her fever goes down. Let's hope she rallies and doesn't go into labour until tomorrow or later."* Soon the nurse arrived with more antibiotics and gave me something to help me sleep.

I woke up at 9:00 pm. when Russ finally arrived. He sat at my side silently - didn't offer any sympathy and finally suggested that I go back to sleep. I drifted off. When I woke up around midnight, the nurse told me that Russ had gone home. I couldn't believe that he'd left me alone, knowing that I might die during the night! How could he care so little about me, that he'd leave me to face my ordeal alone! I realised then, that Russ had never been there when I really needed him. During every crisis in our marriage, I'd had to face things alone. That horrible night I made two stunning disclosures. The first was the confirmation that I'd have to deliver my dead baby alone and secondly - that my marriage was over.

I went into labour and at 5:30 am realised that I had the urge to bear down. I called the nurse who checked me, but said, *"You still have a while to go. I'll check you again in fifteen minutes"* and left the room. Five minutes later I delivered my dead child in my hospital room - alone.

It was 3:00 pm that afternoon before Russ arrived and he wasn't alone. My mother's plane had just arrived. I brushed Russ away and reached for the solace of my mother's arms.

It took me over a year to become strong enough emotionally and physically to leave him. When I did, he swore a vendetta on me (Russ is Italian) that he would take everything I had from me. I moved away with my children, started a new life and stopped his spousal abuse.

Case Study - Papua New Guinea

I have endured several years of emotional, physical, spiritual and sexual abuse provoked by my ex-husband. This violent and abusive "smooth-talking" professional perpetrator also abused our daughter and household pets physically and emotionally and his behaviour continues to this day. He is able to continue his abusive behaviour because he has not been charged or reprimanded by any agency or legal entity. He continues to manipulate and distort facts to individuals that are in a position to take a course of action.

Aided by the interpretation of facts presented by this abusive man, local law enforcement and the court system awarded him temporary custody of our daughter in an on-going custody battle. Aided by "blind justice," this abusive and manipulative individual is using his fine-tuned skills as a perpetrator to get his way and endorse the probability that the abuse will continue.

I have, over the course of this relationship, received a ruptured eardrum, a total of three black eyes, dozens of bruises, countless emotional scars and been forced into the submission of physically painful sexual encounters, to the point of bleeding. In addition to these, I have a permanent mild hearing loss in my left ear as a result of having my eardrum ruptured. I received my first black eye while I was pregnant with our daughter. I was struck hard on the left side of my face by his partially opened right hand. My second beating occurred following an argument over his presumed infidelity and growing pot use. On this occasion I had been drinking and he was under the influence of marijuana. It was following this incident that I went to our local law enforcement, made a statement and showed pictures of my bruises.

When the officer came to the house that evening to question him, he was stoned, but again smooth-talked his way out of it - placing the blame on me for being drunk. Later that night, I was hit again for reporting the abuse and putting him at risk of being caught under the influence of marijuana. I stopped reporting his abusive behaviour, despite several additional occurrences involving my daughter. I changed the locks on the door and filed for divorce.

He sexually abused me on several occasions - following my dumb decision to allow him back into my life following the divorce. The most painful of these occurrences was when I was tied up to my bed and forced to submit to painful anal sex that caused bleeding and discomfort for several days. My husband admitted he was bi-sexual. I also received bruises from being tied up and from his use of handcuffs.

The present day situation has been compounded by my actions and reactions, which I am willing to admit and expand on in this testimony. I allowed this man into my home and into my heart twice. I allowed him back into my life following a divorce. I regret the decision greatly, but take full responsibility for it was a dumb mistake. As my addiction to this relationship escalated, so did my active addiction to alcohol. There is a common notion that 'no one listens to a drunk woman.' I can testify that this is a sad reality and common occurrence in our society.

The emotional abuse was a daily occurrence - insulting, degrading and hurtful remarks said to me and about me, which damaged my self-esteem and confidence. I was told what to do and how to think. My decisions were wrong and my thoughts were invalid if they did not comply with my ex-husband's views. My vocational and educational goals were constantly under attack because our ideals and opinions differed greatly. I now realise that he was attempting to limit my personal growth and success because of his own lack of ambition. I was solely responsible for all costs of the house and household expenses. I was also solely responsible for our daughter's day care and medical costs. At this time, I was also supporting his son from a previous marriage who was living with us.

Our daughter began to think like her father and collaborated with him in the verbal abuse. His ability to control and manipulate our daughter's way of thinking continues to this day.

One Friday, I started drinking at 3:00 pm at home with two six-year-old children in my care. My choice to drink under the circumstances was wrong, but I had hit rock bottom with my alcoholism. Upon reflection, I realise my actions were a desperate cry for help. It stimulated me to obtain treatment and I'm free of my alcohol addiction. I'm actively involved with groups for alcoholism, survivors of abuse and domestic violence and have not taken a drink since that day.

Case study - Diane

I haven't lived with my ex-husband for six years, yet he continues to make my life a living hell. It will never make sense to me that my children have to be constantly uprooted, leave favourite toys and friends behind and look over their shoulders all the time. My three children are innocent bystanders, but they have paid over and over again. They are great kids and they deserve better than living out of a suitcase and being constantly on the run.

I spent one month at a women's centre because it was the only way I could protect myself from him and am continually on the move. My ex-husband had to do three weeks in jail, but his sentence is over and he's back in society. Who is the prisoner here? Certainly not my ex-husband.

I've gone to counselling because I'm so screwed up. We are obtaining help, but sometimes I think I'm too far gone for help, but I'm willing to give it a shot.

Stalking

Case Study – Brisbane

In February 2003, a man was charged by Brisbane's Magistrates Court with stalking and guilty of five breaches of a protection order and was jailed for a month. The 41-year-old spray painter had stalked his former lover and repeatedly told the woman *"I love you."* She had taken a protection order in April, 2002 that banned the man from having contact with her. In August, he was given a three-month suspended sentence, but between October and December he turned up on the woman's doorstep again. The police warned him again. He then confronted the woman in Wintergarden Arcade in Brisbane's Queen Street Mall.

The court was told the man became suicidal but had since completed a domestic violence offender course and anger management course. Brisbane Magistrate Chris Owens said although the man never threatened to use violence he had harassed the woman. *"You have suffered but that is no reason to make her suffer,"* Magistrate Owens said.

Case Study - Pornography

I am 32 years old. I went on my first date with my 43-year-old ex-boyfriend in July, 1999. I agreed to pose for pictures (in various stages of undress and in sexual positions) while we were on a camping trip the summer of 1999 - never guessing they would come back to haunt me. I tried to break it off three months later. This was followed by months of hell and a painful three-year road to justice.

He harassed and threatened me with the pornographic photos taken during our relationship. This is when he started stalking me - sending me letters - some loving and others full of hate and profanity. His annoyances became scary when he threatened to put my pictures on the internet, send them to my family and friends or to my co-workers. I found snapshots left in my mailbox, on my patio door and on my car when it was parked outside my work. But the photographs were only a fraction of my horrifying ordeal. With the photos came a note stating, "You're not afraid for your safety, but fear for your reputation."

I put an alarm system into my home, had friends spend the night and left a photo of my ex with the security desk at work.

He was finally convicted of criminal harassment for the torment I endured through love and hate letters, gifts and lewd pictures. The last unwanted contact I had with him was April 2000 when he breached a restraining order with a phone call.

Police caution anyone willingly posing for permanent, intimate photographic or video evidence to know they risk seeing it used as revenge if the relationship sours.

Case Study - Garry

In April 2003, another man, Garry Paul Stringer, 33, was found guilty of stalking his former girlfriend and charged with assault occasioning bodily harm because of his attack on the male friend of the woman he was stalking. He had been driving while disqualified and was disqualified from driving for three years. He was ordered to surrender the sexually explicit photos he took of his former girlfriend to the police. Stringer was ordered to pay $990 compensation to the man he knocked unconscious and ordered to participate in a domestic violence rehabilitation program and drug and alcohol counselling.

Case Study - Domestic Violence Order

I was subjected to domestic violence for three years in Australia. Getting a domestic violence order (DVO) issued is harder than I thought. I first had to document everything that occurred and fill out form upon form, which is traumatic enough in itself. I then had to appear before a magistrate and was given a temporary order and a court date in a fortnight. Because the local police took 2 ½ months to serve the papers on my ex de facto, it also took 2 ½ months to issue a two-year DVO because my ex de facto needed to appear in court to give his side of the story.

He threatened me at the courthouse and we had to be escorted out by security police via a back entrance. He is currently on the run for more breaches of the DVO. He has already served a 10-day jail sentence as he breached the DVO at least 20 times. These breaches included common assault, home invasion, threatening behaviour, as well as breaching a Family Court Order.

Maybe the police find the current laws take up a huge amount of their time, but that is their job and maybe if certain police officers had done their job more efficiently, my son, my partner and myself wouldn't have to be in hiding away from our friends and family.

We have to constantly look over our shoulders. I did try to solve the problem without running off to the courts, but it didn't work. If you haven't been in a domestic violence situation, you wouldn't even be able to begin to understand. Personally, I think the current domestic violence laws are totally inadequate and, as the saying goes, not worth the paper they're printed on.

Women's Safety, Women's Voices - Office of Women's Policy, Department for Victorian community:

Case Study – Judith

Judith was the twelfth of 13 children. From the age of seven she was sexually molested by her brother. He was fourteen at the time. Judith didn't tell her mother because her brother threatened her.

My brother was Mum's pet. I knew nobody would believe me and didn't talk about it for 53 years". The abuse would occur when her mother was out of the house shopping in the afternoon. The abuse continued until she was 12. It stopped only when her brother, then 19, left home.

She hated her life at home and married at 17. The man she married was later described by his son as "a violent sadist." Judith's story is a catalogue of horrors. "I lived with my husband for 43 years and lived in fear every day.

After she became pregnant with her second child the violence escalated. He husband always had a gun or guns in and around the house. The guns were a constant reminder of the danger she had lived in. He shot at her, menaced her with a shotgun and on two occasions fired weapons at his children. One of the worst beatings she received at his hands was with the butt of a shotgun. Violence was frequent and became routine. In addition, the mental abuse was extreme. On many occasions physical violence would be followed by rape.

As her sons grew he began beating them. Her husband set the two boys up in a boxing match. When they grew tired of it and wanted to stop, he picked up a piece of wood and hit one boy with it, breaking his arm. He then forced the other boy to take the blame.

Judith saw an advertisement in a local newspaper about a public forum on family violence. Almost a year later, Judith went to the domestic violence outreach service. In 1999 her sons, as grown men, joined Judith in laying charges against their father, charges for which he was convicted. For subjecting his family to decades of abuse, he was sentenced to 35 months imprisonment - served 15 months and was released on parole.

Judith has sought out her brother and confronted him with her anger and the misery he caused her by his sexual abuse of her as a child. She now speaks out against violence whenever she has the opportunity and insists that her real name be used.

Conclusion:

Domestic violence is not the preserve of either the economically disadvantages or those in the rural areas. The sooner we put a stop to this widespread domestic abuse, the sooner our homes will truly become the nurturing places they were meant to be. Our women will be able to use their full potential which will lead to enormous economic gains for everyone.

Chapter 6
HOW TO PREVENT AND STOP DOMESTIC VIOLENCE

How couples can resolve battles without violence

Most couples have heated arguments once in a while and some even feel like hitting their spouses at times. This is because they become so frustrated during their exchange that their anger becomes almost intolerable. Most of it stems from the belief that their partner is not listening to them.

Here's a technique that can help couples communicate better during arguments. This communication technique involves trust and faith in each other. Use it when communicating with, spouses, intimate friends and relatives. Participants must agree to abide by the "rules" and see it through.

The ideal time to discuss this technique is when both participants are in a co-operative mood - before the conflict occurs. It won't work if you're already steamed up. So discuss this technique before you have a blow-up.

Have a signal you can use, such as holding your hand up to signify that you want to use the technique. This is how the process works:

1. One person calls a meeting with the other and asks permission to express his or her negative feelings.

2. Only one person talks at a time - the other does nothing but listen and absorb the information until called upon to act.

3. Before the meeting, Person (a) tries to identify what negative childhood tape may be playing (if any) that makes them feel badly about the other person's behaviour.

    Note: Most negative reactions to behaviours of others are reactions from situations that have happened to them as children.

    (i) Person (a) will tell person (b) how s/he feels about issues or something the other's doing that's causing him/her negative feelings.
    (ii) Person (b) will nod to show s/he understands but does not argue or say anything in retaliation.

4. Person (a) makes such statements as *"I feel ... when you do ..."* then explains what s/he wants from the other, *"I need you to ..."*
5. Person (b) then paraphrases as closely as possible, what s/he heard the partner say about the situation, his/her feelings and what s/he wants from him or her.
6. Person (a) then confirms or corrects the information.
7. Person (b) tells Person (a) how s/he feels about what's been said and how s/he intends to deal with it. After Person (a) feels comfortable that s/he's settled the issue, Person (b) may identify one of his/her relationship problems. The process continues until they resolve all their outstanding problems.

There's another way to use this process. One partner would still give the signal (raised hand?) then:

1. Each should write down his or her side of the story.
2. Toss a coin to see who talks first. The person winning the coin toss speaks first.
3. The former listener now becomes the speaker and the new listener follows the same instructions.

The couple has to make a commitment to each other that they will concentrate carefully on what the other person is saying, otherwise the process won't work. They should refrain from formulating any answer to the conflict until it's their turn to speak.

Couples who have used the above procedure find that they truly hear what the other person is saying, (sometimes for the first time). This occurs because they aren't concentrating on formulating their answer. Instead, they concentrate on the other person's side of the story, using empathy to try to understand how the other person really feels about the dispute. The result is open, honest communication between the couple, which settles most conflicts.

However, in the case of abusers, they are seldom willing to listen to what their wives have to say. For those situations, the following will help.

Stopping wife assault

We need a genuine and concerted effort by society, government, business, industry, education, medical and social agencies, as well as individuals (such as you and me) to get to the root cause of violence, to break the cycle. The solution is to enforce zero-tolerance to abuse of any kind whether it is physical, emotional or mental.

It's often difficult for parents who were abused as children, to make the connection between their adult struggle with depression, substance abuse, low self-esteem and their bad childhood relationships. To them, love and not being safe, seem to go together. Those who were abused as children need counselling before they start a relationship and have children. They'd start by:

- Having the courage to acknowledge that they have been abused;
- Heal the damaged child inside themselves so they can become well-balanced and a good parent to their children;
- Get professional help.

Healing is doing hard work on themselves, to remove the pain and confusion. They must take responsibility for their own healing. When they reclaim their personal dignity, their love and spontaneity will return and their anger will dissipate. If they heal those feelings in themselves first, they won't automatically pass bad feelings to their children when under stress.

If they're abusing their children now, they need to get themselves to some kind of facility that can help them control their impulse to abuse. Parents who abuse their children have made a choice not to heal and take care of themselves. Instead, they pass their legacy of pain and confusion onto their children. They can break the cycle by healing themselves first.

One woman I know who was abused as a child, ended up in an abusive relationship and resorted to abusing her children. She had no idea what "normal" family relationships were all about. When she was a child and visited the homes of her girlfriends, she thought the loving relationships she observed in those families were an "act" for her benefit - that the behaviour would be violent when she wasn't there. Only extensive counselling has made her realise that hers was the dysfunctional home.

What do those who have grown up in abusive homes do if they learn that their or their partner's actions are abuse?

- They must get qualified medical help to learn how to deal with the horrific guilt feelings that cling to a person who has had to submit to such aberrant behaviour. They must believe that they were innocent victims of the abuse.

- They must learn how normal families function. They learn this by observing and talking with friends whose families display normal nurturing, loving behaviour. They would ask questions of close friends and seek their help in identifying any reactions to situations or behaviour you're portraying that appears different from how they perceive life.

- Then they need to put their past behind them. What happened in the past - is the past. They need to stop letting it influence everything they do and learn to stop themselves when they find themselves slipping into their former negative thinking.

- They need to set specific realistic goals for themselves and keep telling themselves that they will succeed.

- Write down and remember their successes. They would bring out their "brag list" whenever they're having serious doubts about whether they can succeed or not.

Making the decision to end the cycle of violence is a difficult one for the assaulted woman. Assaulted women cannot stop their partner's violence, however they can stop being victims. These women need to look beyond their own hellish life to the lives of their children because they are not the only ones that the violence cripples and destroys.

Myths and realities of wife battering

Myth #1: Only physical violence is domestic family violence.

Reality: Approsimately only ¼ of DFV is physical – the remaining ¾ is a pattern of behaviour that could be verbally, sexually, emotionally, socially, psychologically or financially abusive; threatening or coercive; or in any other way controlling or seeks to dominate another person that results in living in fear.

Myth #2: If you report DFV your visa will be cancelled and you will be deported.

Reality: Immigration laws in the 'Family Violence Provisions' are intended to ensure that visa applicants (for eligle visa classes) do not need to remain in an abusive relationship in order to get permanent residence in Australia.

Myth #3: If you leave your partner, you will not have financial support.

Reality: Department of Human Servidces, Centreelink supports people affected by family and domestic violenmce if you're in, have left, or are preparing to leave a situation. They provide paymentsd (if eligable), social work counselling and third party referrals. Call 131 202 or visit humanservices.gov.au and select the language button for information in your language.

Myth #4: If you leave there will be no support for you.

Reality: Multicultural Families Organisation (MFO) provides extensive, confidential support for DFV victims including information and advice by a culturally appropriate case worker and can refer you to many other services such as counselling, emergency shelter, financial assistance and free immigration advice. You can contact MFO during business hours.

Myth #5: If you leave you will be homeless.

Reality: Emergency short-term accommodation is available by contacting DV connect for 24/7 support on 1800-811 811.

Myth #6: DFV help is only available if you speak English.

Reality: Every government support service and most other support agencies will provide interpreting services if required. The Translating and Interpreting Service (TIS) provides interpreting services to agencies in 160 languages 24/7. Call 13 14 50.

Myth #7: DFV does not happen in your culture or community.

Reality: DFV is found in all cultures and in all levels of society but the difference is some cultures are making a move to end DFV while in some cultures it is not seen as a problem.

Myth #8: It is your behaviour that caused him to be abusive.

Reality: Abusers choose their actions. Abuse is NEVER the fault of the victim.

Myth #9: For your children, it would benefit them if you stay together.

Reality: All research agrees that children will never benefit in an abusive home where they suffer from emotional and psychological trauma that often leads to physical, social, behavioural and mental health problems. These children are three times more likely to become future abusers or victims of DFV.

Myth #10: Because of your religious beliefs you have to stay in an abusive relationship.

Reality: All mainstream religious writings do not promote or condone DFV. All religious writings and traditions speak about redemption and change from bad to good from suffering to peace and happiness. Marriage if it is full of suffering and abuse must change. If it cannot change, then divorcing a cruel and abusive partner is the appropriate change.

Myth #11: Wife battering is a private matter.

Reality: Wife battering is assault. Assault is a crime. The criminal code defines assault as causing bodily harm to another person or threatening to harm a person. Every citizen has the right to freedom from assault or from fear of assault.

Myth #12: Wife beating is rare.

Reality: It is estimated that there are ten unreported cases for every call by a battered wife to the police.

Myth #13: Family violence is a modern day problem.

Reality: People who have experienced family violence in their childhood tend to accept violence as a method of resolving conflict so family violence continues from generation to generation.

Myth #14: Wife beating occurs infrequently and is rarely severe.

Reality: It is seldom a one-time occurrence. Most battered women are beaten regularly. Most beatings increase in frequency and severity. Beating can lead to permanent physical and mental disability or death. It seldom gets better.

Myth #15: Men beat their wives only when they are drunk. Wife beaters are alcoholics.

Reality: While alcohol and drug abuse are factors in about half the cases of beatings, many men are sober when they assault their wives. Not all drinking or alcoholic men batter their wives.

Myth #16: Women ask for it. They provoke men in quarrels.

Reality: Most women are beaten for no reason and without warning. Stress, conflict, arguments, quarrels and differences are part of any relationship. Pregnancy, added family responsibility and employment problems are key stress factors. Anger and frustration may result. Violence is never an appropriate answer.

Myth #17: Battered wives like it or they would not stay. They must be sick.

Reality: Battered wives stay in relationships for many reasons. Many hope to change a man they love. He may at other times be genuinely penitent, loving and generous. Women may feel they are to blame and try to change. They don't want to admit the marriage is a failure. They feel disloyal, ashamed, isolated or unique. But most of all, women stay because they have nowhere to go. They are trapped.

Myth #18: People don't leave violent relationships. Women are safest when they stay in homes with domestic violence.

Reality: Many leave an average of five to seven times before they are able to leave permanently. Unfortunately, many women are in greater danger from their partner's abuse when they leave. Only they can decide what is best for them and their children. Whether they decide to remain with their abusive partner or leave, it is important they plan for safety.

"Domestic Violence - An Information Book" booklet produced by the Domestic Violence Service Gold Coast (Australia).

Common Questions and Answers:

Question: Is domestic violence a learned behaviour?

Answer: Yes, abusers have often witnessed domestic violence as children. Also, there is widespread tolerance of gender/racial/religious/cultural inequality and violence, that teaches that abuse and controlling behaviour is acceptable. However, abuse that is learned can be un-learned and positive healthy ways of relating can be learned.

Question: Can an abuser change?

Answer: Yes, abusers can change their behaviour, but the process may be slow. It may take a while for them to see the need for reform since it has taken many years for them to develop and normalise their abusive behaviour.

Question: Am I to blame for his violence?

Answer: No. Abusers make a choice to use violence and abuse. They do not "go crazy" or "lose control." They choose who to hurt, when to hurt and how to hurt, to accomplish their ends.

Question: What if he's sorry?

Answer: Most abusers are sorry about their violence afterwards. In fact, remorse is part of the pattern of violence. The abuser may promise to end the violence, to have counselling, buy presents - anything to 'get back to normal.' When the victim returns the pattern of abuse and violence begins again. If an abuser is serious about stopping his violence he will take full responsibility for his behaviour and seek help in changing.

Question: How do I know if he's changed?

Answer: Change comes slowly. Trust your gut feeling regardless of other signs. Ask yourself these questions:

- Has he completely stopped doing and saying things that frighten you?
- Can you express your opinions without fear of being punished?
- Does it feel safe to bring up topics that you know upset him?
- Will he listen to your opinions with respect?
- Does he respect your wishes about sex and physical contact?
- Has he stopped expecting you to do things for him?
- Can you spend time with friends and family without being afraid he will retaliate?
- Do you feel in control of your life?

How safe is your relationship?

The following is a list of warning signals. If you (or someone you know) are with someone new and you notice he has some of these behaviours, it's a possibility that control and abuse may occur. Whether these have happened once or many times, these behaviours indicate this partner is choosing to use a system of power and control. Answering them may alert you to the level of danger in your situation.

- Has your partner verbally abused you now or in the past?

- Has your partner physically assaulted you now or in the past?
- Does your partner have a history of violence?
- Does your partner always see himself as superior or always right?
- Does he use force or coercion to make you do things against your will?
- Does talking to members of the opposite sex result in unfounded jealousy and suspicion that is out of proportion?
- Does your partner need to know where you are constantly?
- Does your partner pressure you to have sex which is unpleasant, pressured or forced?
- Does your partner verbally degrade your self-worth by constantly putting you down?
- Does your partner fail to take responsibility for his actions and/or does he always blame you?
- Does your partner insist that you are always at home or only let you out of the house if they are with you or know where you are going?

Has your partner ever:

- Accused you of having affairs or being sexual with others?
- Acted like you are a possession that can be owned?
- Smashed your belongings or broken things around the house, especially those of value to you?
- Punched holes in the walls or doors?
- Blamed you for his anger and violence, saying it was your fault?
- Monitored or limited your phone calls, conversations and emails?
- Checked the mileage on the car to see if he can work out where you have been or who you have seen?
- Threatened to leave you or told you to leave?
- Kept you from seeing family and friends?
- Taken away your money or controlled how you spend it?
- Refused to pay household bills or give any money towards paying for them?
- Called you fat or ugly or made you feel bad about the way you look?
- Said you were "asking for it" after physically hitting or abusing you?
- Taken away the keys to the car from you?
- Made you do something very humiliating or degrading?

- Used the children to threaten you. For example, told you that you would lose custody or never see the children again?
- Has threatened to, hurt the children, pets, a friend or members of your family or has already done so?
- Insisted you dress more or less sexually than you want?
- Called you a whore, slut or other derogatory names?
- Made you have sex after emotional or physical abuse or when you were sick?
- Tried to control and confuse you with lies?
- Denied all responsibility for his behaviour?
- Pushed, shoved or pulled you?
- Slapped, kicked or punched you?
- Thrown objects at you?
- Spat, urinated of ejaculated on you?

If you have ticked any of these boxes, you are being abused - domestic violence is happening in your relationship. You are entitled to be safe. The more often you answered "yes" - the greater risk you are in.

Safety Planning

It may be helpful to set up some safety plans for you and your children. It is important that you don't let your partner see the plan, but it is a good idea to talk about it with someone you trust who is close to you.

This safety plan has three parts:

- To avoid serious injury and escape violence;
- To separate safely;
- To plan for long-term safety after separation.

Avoid serious injury and escape violence

- During an incident of violence at home, you will want to do everything you can to avoid serious injury:
- Leave if you can;
- Know the easiest escape routes – doors, windows etc.;
- Know where you're going to go;
- Have a safe place arranged that is known to you and your children if possible;

- Identify a neighbour you can tell about the violence and ask them to call the police if they hear a disturbance coming from your house.
- Develop a code between you;
- Teach the children to call the police emergency number and practice what to say;
- Have the phone number of your nearest women's shelter memorised or easy to find.

Leaving Safely

Determine where you will go for safety; friends, family or women's shelter. Always try to take the children with you. Keep a small amount of cash to make emergency calls, key cards, keys, essential medications and important papers together in a place where you can get them quickly or have someone else retrieve them. You may wish to have a copy of these left with someone you trust. Remember, if you do leave, you can always request police to accompany you back to the house to get your personal possessions.

Make your own list (birth and marriage certificates, copies of Domestic Violence Orders, custody papers, passports, any identification papers, drivers licence, insurance policies, work and income documents, medicare number, private insurance number, unemployment insurance number, employee tax file number, bank account details and statements, cheque book, credit cards, immigration documentation, adoption papers, medical and legal records, etc.)

- Arrange transport in advance.
- Ask your family doctor to carefully note any evidence of injuries on your patient records. Include coloured photographs of injuries if at all possible.
- Inform your children's school and day care who has permission to collect the children.
- Review your banking and postal arrangements.
- Review your safety plan. Remember that leaving can be your most dangerous time.

Long-term safety after separation

- If possible, use different shops and banks to those you used previously.
- Consider installing an outside sensor lighting system.

- Change locks and ensure window security. A security chain could be fitted to all entry doors and used at all times when the door is answered by you or your children.
- Plan for extra safety between leaving your car and entering your home, e.g. an automatic garage door opener, safety lighting or removal of shrubs or trees in the area.
- Vary your travel routes to and from work. Keep map handy and pre-plan routes in unknown areas to prevent you from having to leave your vehicle.
- Tell neighbours that your partner does not live with you and ask them to call the police if he is seen near your home or if they hear an assault occurring.
- Tell your employer that you have a protection order or that you are afraid of your ex-partner and ask for your telephone calls at work to be screened.
- If your ex-partner breaches the protection order, telephone the police and report the breach. If the Police do not help, contact your advocate or a legal service for assistance to make a complaint.
- Ask your telephone company about the installation of "caller ID" on your telephone and ask for an unlisted number.
- Contact your local electoral commission and ask for your name and address to be excluded from the published electoral role.
- Attend a woman's education program to help you grow stronger and understand what has happened to you.

Legal issues

What is a Protection Order?

A Protection Order is an order made by the Magistrate's Court under the Domestic and Family Violence Protection act 1989. This legislation is civil legislation meaning that no criminal offence is recorded until a respondent to the order has been charged and convicted on a breach of the order. Under the legislation, applications can be brought before the court by police, an aggrieved person or someone acting on their behalf. There is no fee for lodging an application.

Domestic Violence Service staff are available to discuss applications with you or advocate with police or other agencies on your behalf. A police prosecutor is available to represent you in court, but you must request this at the time of lodging the original application. In serious circumstances, a temporary protection order may be issued until a final decision on the application has been made. All orders (either temporary or final) will need to be served on the abusing partner who has the right under the law to come to court and either consent or contest the application. If the application is contested, it is then set down for hearing.

As the rules of evidence in civil matters are different - based on the balance of probabilities - then you can consider what may be of assistance to progress your application - these could include medical reports, photos of injuries or damage to property and statements from witnesses.

How will the protection order work?

The court can impose a number of directions, which a respondent must obey. The basic protection order has four sets of conditions stating; that the respondent spouse should be of good behaviour and not commit an act of domestic violence towards the aggrieved spouse and any aggrieved persons named on the order. It also states that the respondent may not possess weapons for the duration of the order and all weapon licenses must be cancelled.

This allows contact between both parties. If you wish to have no contact with your partner/ex-partner, then there is provision to add specific conditions either when first applying for the order or at any stage while the order is still current.

How to report a breach of order

A breach occurs when the respondent either personally or through another person, does any act, which disobeys any of the conditions on the order. It needs to be proven that the respondent knew about the order and the conditions of the order before they can be charged in court.

If you believe that your order has been breached, record all details. Try to keep as much evidence as possible:

- What happened?
- When and where it happened?
- Were there any witnesses?

If the police charge the respondent with a breach of the Protection Order, they are arrested and brought before a Magistrate at the courthouse. If the respondents plead guilty, they will be sentenced.

Depending on the seriousness of the breach, they will probably be given a fine and after repeated breaches they may get a prison sentence. If the respondent pleads not guilty, the matter will be sent to a trial or hearing. If the matter is sent to trial, you will be required to give evidence at court.

The court can impose a number of directions that a respondent must obey. These can include not coming to your place of residence or work, not to contact you or commit further acts of violence. It will also require the person to surrender firearms and firearm licences. If the Protection Order is breached or ignored and the person named on it tries to contact you in any way, you must report it to the police. The abuser is liable to be arrested, go to prison or face a large fine. It is a criminal offence to breach a Domestic Violence Order. It's important to keep several copies of your order and keep them in a safe place.

Conclusion:

There is greater awareness about domestic violence as a result of sustained campaigns by various bodies. More people are willing to speak about it and start to seek solutions. Crime Stoppers have made it possible for people to report suspected domestic violence and child abuse to authorities with complete anonymity. Counselling facilities are improving, but legislation is lagging decades behind the times. This is a battle that must be fought and won, for the good of the millions who are victims of abuse not only in our country, but world-wide.

What can witnesses do?

If you see an assault in progress - take action. Find the nearest phone and call the police. Don't assume that someone else has done so. If you are in your car, honk your horn until a group gathers, he stops hitting her or the police come. These situations can be dangerous, so whatever you do, be sure to keep yourself safe. But *do* take action. At the very least, watch them. By being a witness in a way that lets him know that you see him, you may reduce the level of violence.

If someone you know is using violence:

1. Call the police. This is criminal behaviour and we do not help abusive men by playing down the seriousness of their abuse. Once they have been held accountable, family and friends can help him

to choose non-violent alternatives and check on the safety of women and children.
2. If you or someone you know has influence with the abusive person, you may be able to talk to him about his behaviour provided it seems safe to do so.
3. When talking with the man, it is important to stress that the discussions stem from personal observations, not from what his partner may have told you, as this will severely compromise her safety.
4. It may be helpful to talk to someone who knows and understands domestic violence and listen to his or her suggestions. This will help to keep those involved safe.

Why do friends and family not offer help?

"I shouldn't get involved in a private family matter."
"She must be doing something to provoke his violence."
"If it was really bad, she would just leave."
"Doesn't she care about what's happening to her children?"
"I know him - I really don't think he could hurt anyone."
"How can she still care for someone who abuses her?"
"If she needs my help - she'd ask for it."

(From *Wife Assault - Hurts all of us* brochure prepared by Frances Cearns, Lenore Walker, Karen Neilsen and Edmonton Area Inter-Agency Committee on Wife Assault Services (Canada)

Laying assault charges

When the abused woman decides to break her cycle of violence, she also assumes responsibility for following through with her decisions. Nowhere is this clearer than in laying charges of assault.

Assault is a criminal code offence. When there is physical evidence that an assault has occurred, it is the job of police to lay charges against the offender. Where no physical evidence of assault exists, laying a charge of assault may become the responsibility of the victim.

It's unfair that police cannot remove the offender from the home, but will assist the assaulted women and her children to leave. Assisting victims to get to safe houses is the only way police have to guarantee their safety, because offenders are often released within 24 hours and can return home. Police are then powerless to protect victims who choose to remain in their homes.

[Author's Comments] This is where the laws need changing. Why should the innocent victims (wives and children) be forced to leave their home and the assaulter allowed to stay? Accusers should be forced to leave the home and have restraining orders placed on them to stay away from their wives and children. In cases of serious battering, they should be given jail sentences related to the level of abuse and forced to attend counselling sessions until the counsellor believes they have changed.

Assaulted women are usually required to appear in court to testify. Shelter workers, court workers and victim service units should guide the assaulted woman through the legal system. [End of Author's Comments].

Building a support network

Taking responsibility for herself and her children can seem overwhelming for an abused woman. Developing a support network can help the assaulted woman understand wife assault and learn skills to cope with the problems she will encounter leaving or staying in the relationship. For the woman who chooses to remain in her abusive relationship, a support network can act as an escape plan if the time comes to leave her abusive partner. Abused women need to know that they are not alone in their attempts to deal with their partners' violence. Shelter workers and counsellors understand that the effects of wife assault such as lowered self-esteem, self-blame and guilt often prevent victims from reaching out for help. They are prepared to work though these problems with victims by providing the emotional support they need. Many abused women report that once they reach out and connect with a support network, they feel less like victims and more like survivors.

Many abused women find the only way to ensure their own safety is to leave the relationship. It becomes easier to reach out for help from others when she is not constantly fearful of further abuse. Often women plan to leave temporarily until they or their partners seek help. Women report that following through with counselling, decisions become easier when the stress of living with the abuse is removed.

National Register

At long last a national domestic violence register has been set up to protect battered women and children after Australia's attorneys general declared it was a top priority.

The national register allows police anywhere in Australia to quickly identify men who have a history of beating their partners or children. Women who leave abusive relationships by moving interstate won't need to apply for a new set of protection orders in the state or territory where they live.

Shelters

Shelters and second-stage housing provide a safe, nurturing environment for survivors and their children. While at the shelters, women can gather information, receive support, make decisions and access available community resources. Women have a chance to share their experiences with others from similar situations in an atmosphere supervised by staff who are knowledgeable, caring and non-judgemental. For women and children to be with others from similar situations helps them to let go of their fear, shame and isolation.

The shelters operate as crisis services and stays are short-term (three weeks on average). Facilities known as second-stage housing provide a longer stay (four to six months) for families who require more intensive support and security. Shelters and second-stage houses provide different levels of child support services.

Counselling

Counsellors have an obligation to ensure that the abused woman's safety is considered at all times. In cases where violence has occurred and the fear of further violence is present, counsellors have found that the woman's safety and the abusive man's responsibility for the violent act, are most clearly established when the victim and offender are seen in counselling separately - rather than as a couple. Sometimes information disclosed in counselling can trigger abuse and so couple counselling is chosen only after it has been established that the violence and threats of violence have stopped and the likelihood of future violence is reduced.

When choosing a counsellor it's important to select someone with knowledge of wife assault. If a client is not comfortable or satisfied with the counsellor's skills, a more appropriate counsellor should be found. Some women are more at ease with a female counsellor than a male. Some agencies offer individual and/or group counselling. It's important that the abused woman's needs and preferences are made known to the counsellor. Private therapists may have a sliding fee scale with rates based on the client's ability to pay. Abused women are encouraged to question the training and helping methods of the counsellors they choose.

Assaulted women's support groups are being offered in various agencies. These groups give women a chance to strengthen their support networks, share their problems and evaluate available community resources. Some groups have been ongoing and membership is on a drop-in-basis. Others are more structured and have a definite beginning and end point. Information is available from intake workers at these agencies.

Building a support network through a support group is an effective way of coping as a survivor of wife assault. Support can help women through the difficult times whether they decide to return to their relationships or to remain on their own. The support gained from these groups helps reinforce the reality of the woman's experiences and feelings and strengthens her belief in her worth and her right to live without violence.

Legal Resources

Legal Aid gives access to legal counsel at a reduced rate of payment. Once a woman qualifies for Legal Aid, her first appointment is with an intake worker. This person takes information and a lawyer is assigned to help her. This may take several days to one week. A client deals directly with that lawyer once legal counsel is assigned. Women whose incomes prevent them from qualifying for Legal Aid may have to seek independent legal counsel. Lawyer Referral services provides names of lawyers who know about wife assault. Student Legal Services can provide information (not legal counsel) that may assist in determining if a lawyer is needed for a particular legal action. The service is usually free.

When there are concerns that children are at risk from harm or abduction from an abusive partner, Family Court can help obtain custody to protect children at risk. There are various types of custody orders that can be granted, depending on the particular situation. An intake worker at Family Court can explain the custody options. An appointment is made with a Family Court counsellor. This counsellor assesses the situation and gives advice about appropriate action. This service is also usually free.

Shelters: [Author's Comments]

Community programs that offer education, support and relief for parents can help prevent child abuse. Treatment programs for abusers and potential abusers can help, as can educating children about abuse.

The most significant change that has occurred to help battered women is the formation of "safe" houses where they can go (often with their children) to get away from their battered husbands. They provide a home where a woman with her child(ren) may go if she and/or her children are beaten or are under threat of violence by her husband or common-law partner. It provides a secure and supportive atmosphere where a woman can make decisions for her family's future. Along with food, shelter and emergency necessities, women's shelters provide:

- Emotional support in a period of social and personal change.
- Referral services to social agencies for legal, financial, marriage, family and health counselling.
- A maintenance educational program for children of school age.
- Regular visits from nurses to deal with any health issues.
- Regular visits and discussions with lawyers.
- Trained child support workers to assist children.
- Follow-up workers to assist families in settling into the community after they leave the shelter.

In 2003 of the 337 children who accompanied their mothers to the shelter, the majority were abused in some manner:

- Nine out of ten children, between 13 and 18;
- Two-thirds of the infants were seriously abused or neglected;
- One-third of the children between 11 and 18 had been sexually abused;
- One-third of all identified sexual abuse victims were boys;
- One-half of the abused children displayed behavioural and emotional problems severe enough to require referral to treatment agencies.

Children do not need to be physically or sexually assaulted, to be hurt by wife abuse. Those who witness violence in the home are also victims. Young children who watch violence between their parents can react with behaviours such as shaking, crying, poor sleeping patterns and recurring nightmares, bed-wetting, stuttering and clinging to parents. Older children sometimes show effects similar to those of women who are psychologically abused such as lowered self-esteem, self-blame, drug and alcohol abuse and aggressiveness.

Most children feel responsible for the violence in the family. They blame themselves for everyone's unhappiness and suffering. It's a shame that society and the judicial system see acts of violence towards women and children as criminal acts and yet the victims of such acts feel like they are the criminals? The workers at women's shelters do their best to convince them that what happened to them was not their fault but the fault of their abusive partner.

These battered women's shelters are in dire need of contributions for both the women and their children. Many flee their abuser with nothing but the clothing on their backs (often pajamas and nightgowns). So they need all the items that a person would normally take in a suitcase if they expect to leave home for a month or so. [End of Author's Comments]

Women's Safety Strategy (Office of Women's Policy - Department for Victorian Communities).

The Government has a vision for a safer future for all Victorians. In Growing Victoria Together the Government has outlined its commitment to safer streets, homes and workplaces. A Crime and Violence Prevention Strategy has been developed. Local Safety Committees exist in each municipality. Police, local government, community organisations and others are all working to improve safety.

Despite significant advances for women over the past 30 years, many women continue to live in fear and violence. More than one in three Australian women has experienced violence or a serious threat of violence in their adult lives. One quarter of young people have witnessed physical abuse against their mother or stepmother.

In Victoria, police attend over 20,000 incidents of family violence each year. Victoria Police recorded rapes or sexual assaults against nearly 4,000 Victorian women or girls each year. National research shows that the true extent of violence against women is far greater. Over 80% of violence against women is not reported to the police or other services.

(This extensive policy framework covers the following headings):

- A safety strategy for women;
- Working together;
- A shared understanding of violence against women;
- Addressing violence against women;
- Appendix 1: Victorian Government roles and responsibilities in relation to women's safety;
- Appendix 2: Members of the Women's Safety;
- Co-ordinating Committee (WSCC).

Implementation of the Strategy

The Women's Safety Strategy is an overarching policy framework to guide the work of Departments in addressing violence against women. Responsibility for planning and implementing initiatives rests with individual departments. Within this framework, a number of mechanisms have been established to ensure a high level of co-ordination.

- There will be an Annual Meeting of Minister on Women's Safety to set priorities and monitor progress.
- Three steering committees are also being established to provide advice in relation to the implementation of the Women's Safety Strategy in the following key areas:
  - Statewide Steering Committee to Reduce Family Violence;
  - Statewide Steering Committee to Reduce Sexual Assault and Non-relationship;
  - Violence Against Women;
  - Statewide Steering Committee to Reduce Violence Against Women in the Workplace.
- Sexual violence will be included in the work of each of the three committees. This acknowledges that sexual violence may occur in various settings and that the relationship of the perpetrator to the victim/survivor may range from partner, ex-partner or family member to work colleague, acquaintance or stranger.
- The steering committees will have both Government and non-government representatives. They will ensure a high level of consultation and co-ordination across Government Departments and between the Government and non-government sectors. These

- committees will report to the Chief Commissioner of Police and will provide direct advice to government Departments through Departmental representatives on the Committee.
- The implementation plan includes a number of initiatives being undertaken jointly as a partnership between two or more Departments. It is expected that the number of joint initiatives will increase over the life of the Strategy.

To order one of their extensive kits for ***Women's Safety Strategy*** contact owp@dpc.vic.gov.au

Australian assistance

Victims Referral And Assistance Service
GPO Box 4356QQ
Melbourne, VIC 3001
Ph: (03) 9603-9797 or
1800 819 817

Victim Support Service
11 Halifax Street,
Adelaide, S.A. 5000
Ph: (08) 8231-5626
1800 182 368

Victims of Crime Bureau
Level 6, 299 Elizabeth St,
Sydney, NSW 2000
Ph: (02) 9374-3000
1800 633 063

Assisting Victims of Crime,
6th Floor, 81 St. George's Terrace,
Perth, WA 6000
Ph: (09) 322-3711
1800 818 988

Victims of Crime Association
5 Croydon Road,
Woodridge, Queensland 4114
Ph: (07) 3290-2513 (Brisbane)

1300 733 777 (24 hr support)

Victims of Crime Assistance League (VOCAL)
1 Lluka Street,
Narrabundah ACT 2604
(02) 6295-9600

Victims of Crime Assistance League (VOCAL),
Ph: (02) 9374-1636 (Sydney)
Ph: (02) 9426-5826 (Newcastle

Lifeline (sponsored by the Uniting Church - Sunshine Coast)
Ph: 13 11 14
Victims of Crime Service,
160 New Town Road,
New Town, Tasmania 7008
Ph: (03) 6228-7628

Victims of Crime Assistance League (VOCAL)
43 Mitchell Street,
Darwin, NT 0800
Ph: 1800 672 242 (24 hours)

Domestic violence regional services

Here is a listing of the domestic violence services that are available in Queensland. All states would have similar lists should you want to learn where the nearest domestic violence service is in your area:

Brisbane Domestic Violence Advocacy Service
Ph: (07) 3217-2544
Fax: (07) 3217-2679

Domestic Violence service Gold Coast
Ph: (07) 5532-9000
Fax: (07) 5571-1508

Caboolture Regional Domestic Violence Service inc.
Ph: (07) 5498-9533
Fax: (07) 5498-9530

Domestic Violence Regional Service (South West)
Ph: (07) 4639-3605
Fax: (07) 4639-6887

North Queensland Domestic Violence
Resource Centers
Ph: (07) 4721-2888
Fax: (07) 4721-1794

The Domestic Violence Service of Central Queensland
Ph: (07) 4982-4288
Fax: (07) 4987-5448

Domestic Violence Service (Far South West)
Ph: (07) 4622-5230
Fax: (07) 4622-5320
Cairns Regional Domestic Violence Service
Ph: (07) 4040-6100
Fax: (07) 4040-6111

Suncoast / Cooloola / Outreach Prevention &Education Domestic & Family Violence
Services for Safer Communities
Ph: (07) 5479-5911
Fax: (07) 5479-5907

Ipswich Women's Centre Against Domestic Violence
Ph: (07) 3816-3000
Fax: (07) 3816-3100

WAVSS Logan
Ph: (07) 3808-5566
Fax: (07) 3808-5109

Domestic Violence Resource Service (Mackay & Region)
Ph: (07) 4957-3888
Fax: (07) 4957-3984

Coordinated Community Response to Domestic Violence, Wynnum
Ph: (07) 3348-3867
Fax: (07) 3393-5080

Redlands Domestic Violence Service (Maybanks Inc.)
Ph: (07) 3820-2114

Domestic Violence Service Gold Coast
Crisis: Ph: 5532-9000
Admin: Ph: 07 5591-4222
Fax: (07) 5571-1508
admin@domesticviolence.com.au

If you or a family member are experiencing family violence, a life is being threatened or there's an emergency please call police on **triple zero (000).**

For further assistance contact domestic violence helplines:

DVConnect Womensline:
1800 811 811
24 hours, 7 days a week

DVConnect Mensline:
1800 600 636
9am-midnight 7 days a week

Women's Legal Service:
Regional 1800 677 278
Brisbane (07) 3392 0670

Kids Helpline:
For young people up to the age of 25 (free call)

Child Safety after hours:
1800 177 13
24 hours (for concerns about children)

Elder Abuse

25,000 older Queenslanders are abused yearly by someone they trust. Elder abuse occurs when someone who is in a position of trust neglects or causes emotional, social, financial, physical or sexual harm to an older person. This could include a family member, a friend or someone with a "power of attorney."

The Elder Abuse Prevention Unit operates a confidential telephone Helpline for people who witness or experience abuse or fear they may be responsible for elder abuse. Callers can choose to remain anonymous. By calling Helpline, you can talk about the situation and explore the options that are available. The caller is always free to act on any, all or none of the options identified in their conversation Helpline.

Helpline operates 9:00 am – 5:00 pm weekdays at 1300 651 192.

www.eapu.com.au The Elder Abuse Prevention Unit also provides awareness raising talks to any community group or organisation involving older people and their families.

Reporting abuse

Why don't targets of abuse report that abuse? There are many reasons;

- Abuse is a betrayal; the target trusted and depended on the integrity of another person and that person betrayed them. The target fears and anticipates that if they report the abuse, they will be betrayed again.
- Those in authority did nothing to prevent the abuse while it was happening, nor did they do anything subsequently. Very often it was a person in the position of authority who was the abuser. Trust in authority is low, with justification.
- The target fears, with justification, that no one will believe them.
- Disbelief and denial are everywhere. People not trained in abuse and with no experience of dealing with abuse find it easier to disbelieve and deny the abuse.
- If the target reports the abuse and initiates legal action, prospects for future employment may be impaired.
- Abusers often operate in networks, sharing information and even, in paedophilia, sharing victims. Sometimes the networks are loose, but sometimes they operate covertly within organisations.
- The abuser relies on compulsive lying - Jekyll and Hyde nature. They are charming and use denial, counter-attack and projection and feigning victim hood to evade accountability. Their charm has a motive - deception.
- The target felt fear at the time of the abuse and continues to feel fear - fear of violence, fear of losing her job, fear of humiliation and fear of what others will think.
- The target feels ashamed of what happened, having been encouraged by the abuser to believe that she was responsible, rather than the abuser being responsible.
- Because abuse can be of an intimate nature (such as sexual abuse), the target feels embarrassed about what happened and continues to feel embarrassed talking about it.
- The target felt and continues to feel guilty about what happened, having been encouraged by her abuser to believe she was at least partly responsible.
- Fear, shame, embarrassment and guilt are how all abusers control their victims by their power.
- The target probably has unusually high levels of naivety that are heightened by the trauma that the abuser continues to exploit. The

target may have been encouraged to withdraw from legal action by the abuser feigning victim hood. They play on their target's forgiving nature and other people's sympathies for the abuser to gain absolution for their actions.
- The target feels bewildered and often still cannot believe that it happened. The target often feels responsible in some way, as evidenced by the nagging thought, *"Why did I let it happen to me?"*
- Abuse causes trauma that prevents the target articulating what is happening to them.
- Trauma and fear also prevent the target from being able to find the right words to identify, unmask and call to account the tormenter.
- Abuse causes Post Traumatic Stress Disorder (PTSD) and any thought, memory or reminder of the abuse immediately results in the sufferer experiencing intense psychological and physiological distress.

How to help a battered woman

Listen to her. Be supportive and understanding. Let her know she is not alone or to blame. Do not be judgemental. Suggest she go to a doctor as soon as possible following the beating. She should tell the doctor the cause of her injuries, as she may need medical evidence later. Coloured photographs of her injuries may be vital evidence in court.

If you witnessed the battering or saw her directly afterward, be willing to act as a witness in court.

If she plans to leave her home, remind her to take legal identification. If she wants to leave and has nowhere to go, suggest she contact her nearest women's shelter. If she's undecided what to do, suggest she at least call the women's shelter for advice. They provide battered women with reliable information about counselling, legal and social assistance available to her.

You can help her to start a new life by helping her find a job, housing and childcare. Remember, what she does is her decision. It's her life. Many women have been in this situation and have made new, violence-free lives for themselves. Regardless of her decision, remember she needs emotional support during this difficult period of her life.

Conclusion:

Matters of assault and battery should not be taken lightly by either the victims or those close to them who witness or are aware of the abuse. Besides ongoing legal reforms, societal attitudes that view women as property or that stigmatises a woman's leaving her marital home for any reason, need to change.

Chapter 7
DEALING WITH RAPE AND STALKERS

Adult rape victims

Rape, whether it's of a male or a female, is a terrifying act to the victim, no matter at what age the outrage took place. Most suffer from Post-Traumatic Stress Disorder (PTSD) at least in the beginning. Almost twenty per cent of raped women never completely get rid of their PTSD symptoms.

The survey found that many more women were subjected to unwanted sexual events than were reported to police and/or community crime surveys.

Victims who felt they were in great physical danger during the rape were more likely to get severe PTSD than those who felt they were in less danger. If threatened with a weapon or raped by a stranger, they were more likely to get severe PTSD. Date rape often carries more physical violence for women. This is because the woman has a greater sense of security. After all, she knows the man and she is more likely to resist and fight back. The result can be a severe beating.

Others felt they had set themselves up for rape by "doing something dumb" so suffered from feelings of guilt and shame. Those who were raped when they felt they had "done everything right" suffered greater anxiety because they saw the world as an unsafe place.

Some victims don't tell anybody because they're afraid others will blame them for the rape. They have not compared their assault to other crimes. For instance, nobody would believe them or that they had "asked for it," if they were the victims of a robbery or if they were physically assaulted. Nobody wants to hear about a rape. The message seems to be, *"Don't talk about it."*

According to Queensland University of Technology research, women are reluctant to discuss unwanted sexual events because often they:

- Felt guilty or embarrassed;
- Considered it a private matter;
- Feared reprisals;
- Did not think they would be taken seriously; or
- Feared the court process.

Dealing with Domestic Violence and Child Abuse

The survey found that about:

- 80 per cent of women have experienced some form of sexual violence or harassment during their life;
- 19 per cent of women had experienced attempted rape;
- 13 per cent had been raped;
- 40 per cent had had sex due to overwhelming arguments;
- 46 per cent had given in to sex play when they did not want to;
- 25 per cent of the women reported unwanted events where someone had tried to arouse them;
- 34 per cent said someone had exposed themselves to them; and
- 25 per cent said they had been forced to arouse someone else.

How victims can be assisted:

Experts in this area advise that helping the victim re-experience the rape by talking about it, imagining it, re-creating it in their mind, is the best treatment. Most reveal that they have recurring night-mares, flashbacks and endless thoughts of how they could have handled the event better.

- After a few weeks, most can resume near-normal lives. They're better prepared to deal with issues that were frightening to them, such as going to places that they perceive are threatening or sleeping alone in their home.
- The rubber band on the wrist is a helpful technique. When they find themselves dwelling on the event, they snap the band, which gives their subconscious mind a jolt to keep it from going back to the negative thoughts.
- Give them instruction on how they can manage future anxiety. For example, they may have to deal with sudden anxiety, if they see someone who resembles the criminal who committed the crime.
- Offer counselling that can help the victim handle everyday events.
- Encourage them to take self-defence courses.

Date Rape

One study presented at the American Psychological Association suggest that 28 per cent of dating relationships contain some kind of physical, emotional or sexual abuse against women. The Stockholm Syndrome might be even more likely to develop in young women's dating relationships. One reason is that young women are more likely to perceive violence as signs of love. Young men in dating relationships tend to receive a lot of peer support for exhibiting behaviour that's masculine, aggressive and meant to control women.

- One in ten high school students have experienced some form of abuse in their dating relationships.
- One in eight women living with a male partner experiences some kind of abuse.
- At some time during their lives, one in four females and one in three males have been victims of unwanted sexual acts.
- Sixty-two per cent of all women murdered are victims of domestic violence.
- Wife abuse is rarely a one-time occurrence. Each incident reduces the abuser's internal control and makes it more likely that another incident will occur. The more it happens, the more likely it is to happen again.
- Beatings are frequently severe. About one-third of cases, medical treatment is required. Injuries include bruises, lacerations, fractures, burns, dislocations and scalds. Women have been attacked with fists, boots, broken bottles, knives, razors and belt buckles.
- Wife abuse frequently happens after hours. Seventy per cent of reported assaults occur between 5:00 pm and 7:00 am. About half the incidents occur on weekends.

Dating abuse

Usually when we think of abuse and assault (battering) we think of it in physical terms - being hit, kicked or punched or maybe "just" slapped around:

> *"He never really hit me, he just used to push me against the wall and he only pushed me down once."*

Not all abuse is physical. There are kinds that leave no marks. They are psychological and emotional abuse. This kind of abuse can take many forms, from being put down in little ways, being told that you're ugly, fat or stupid, to being bugged and harassed into doing something that

Dealing with Domestic Violence and Child Abuse

you may not have wanted. This kind of abuse usually happens when you are isolated or when you don't spend time with other friends or family. It's important to have somebody to talk to - as a reality check - when you are being told this about yourself. It's so much harder to recognise and talk about, because there are no visible signs

> *"He thought my friends were too young, so we always partied and hung around with his friends. The first time we broke up, I noticed none of my friends were left."*

Boyfriends who do or say these kinds of things are trying to control you and keep you from being independent. Remember that neither they nor anybody else has that right.

Another kind of abuse is forced sexual contact or intimacy. Sometimes you might start a sexual relationship with your boyfriend because you think that you might lose them if you didn't. It can mean being cajoled and pleaded with - so you feel guilty - to being actually forced. It's your right to decide when and how you want sex. When your boyfriend ignores this, it amounts to harassment, physical assault and rape. It's your right to say "no" and mean it

> *"I said I didn't want to fool around. He called me a tease."*
> *"It seemed like he didn't listen when I told him I didn't like it."*
> *"I gave in. I didn't want to fight about it any more."*
> *"I thought that if I didn't go along, he wouldn't love me any more."*

There are many reasons why you might not walk away from a relationship. There is a lot of social pressure to have a boyfriend take you to parties or just to go out with. If you don't have a boyfriend, people sometimes think there is something wrong with you or sometimes even see you as threatening; that you're not okay. Sometimes staying with a boyfriend who batters you is less frightening than being alone in a society that measures your worth by whether you have a partner or not.

> *"Everybody thinks he's such a hunk, they don't know what he's really like."*
> *"Whenever I cried, he'd always tell me he could go out with any other girl and I'd better shut up or he would. I believed him."*
> *"He was so jealous about everybody that I looked at. For a long time, I thought that it meant he loved me."*

A woman who is lonely or isolated is more susceptible to battering, because she has no one to talk with. She can feel that her boyfriend is the only one that loves and cares about her. This makes his behaviour even more confusing and she may start to feel that she deserves what he is doing to her. Her self-esteem slowly deteriorates to the point where he has a great deal of power over her and she may start to believe that she deserve the battering. Nobody does!

Many women feel that it is their fault the relationship is not working because their boyfriends told them so. They feel that it is their responsibility to try harder to understand and love more. They try to change it by themselves. It takes a long time to realise that it's their boyfriends who must change their behaviour and they can't do it for them.

> "I thought that if I loved him enough, he would change."
> "I love him more than anything in the world and I try so hard to be what he wants."
> "It took me a long time to figure out that his temper had nothing to do with me. I couldn't change it."

Battering happens to many people whether others see it or not. You are not alone. There are problems and stresses within every relationship. Battering in whatever form is not an okay way to work things out and it's not something you should accept. Nobody deserves to be abused.

> "He slapped me around one time when he thought I was after his best friend. We were just talking."

The best way to stop abuse is by not accepting it; telling your boyfriend or date that it's not all right with you or leaving. Staying in the situation is not going to help anybody and he may not even realise that his behaviour is wrong. Too often women believe that it's their responsibility as nurturers to stay and help keep the relationship together. But as long as they stay, their boyfriends have no reason to change.

> "They all thought I was stupid to go out with him. They didn't know how much we loved each other."

Conclusion:

The best way to stop dating abuse is by not accepting it. Tell your boyfriend or date that it is ***not*** all right with you and leave if they do not change. Staying in the situation is not going to help anybody and he may not even realise that his behaviour is wrong.

Talk to somebody - a friend, counsellor or a women's group. There are lots of people who don't understand or who may not even want to know. Don't be discouraged if you find one of them. Keep on trying. There are people who care. Nobody deserves that. There is always a way out.

Dealing with Stalkers

(From the book: I Know You Really Love Me (Dell, 1998) written by Doreen Orion, MD).

Stalking victims don't like to be called victims. They will say, "I won't let myself be victimised," or, *"I'm not going to change my life because I'm being stalked."* Sorry. Your life has changed. Forever. Unless you accept that, you will actually be helping the stalker. You are a crime victim. The crime happens to be stalking. You must understand that the phrase "stalking victim" says volumes about the perpetrator, but nothing about you. It does not tell us whether you stay at home in terror with sheets over the windows or whether you've decided to move or to become active to change the laws in your state. On the other hand, accepting that you are a stalking victim serves to remind you that you must, from now on, take extra precautions that others do not have to take.

Here are some basics to start with:

1. Tell the stalker *"No"* once and only once and then never give him the satisfaction of a reaction again. The more you respond, the more you teach him that his actions will elicit a response. This only serves to reinforce the stalking.
2. Get a dog. The Los Angeles Police Department's Threat Management Unit says this is *"one of the least expensive but most effective alarm systems."*
3. Block your address at DMV and Voter Registration. If you don't, anyone can get it for the asking.
4. Never give out your home address or telephone number. Get a post office box and use it on all correspondence. For those places that will not accept a post office box, change "PO Box" to Apt." and leave the number. Put this address on your cheques.
5. When the stalker gets your home telephone number, don't change it. Instead, always let an answering machine pick up. Get a new, unlisted number and give it to everyone who calls but the stalker.

Gradually, only your stalker will be using your old number - it will become his private line. If it upsets you when he calls, put the machine in a room you don't use. You can even have someone else monitor the tapes. This way, the stalker will think he is still getting through to you, although you will never make the mistake of picking up when he calls. Whenever you close off one avenue for a stalker, he will find another and it could easily be worse.

6. Document everything. Even if you have decided not to go the legal route, you may change your mind. Keep answering machine tapes, letters, gifts, etc. Keep a log of drive-bys or any suspicious occurrences.
7. Take a self-defence class. A lot of security experts don't advise this, fearing that it gives victims a false sense of security - but we do. The best self-defence classes teach you how to become more aware of your surroundings and avoid confrontations, things that stalking victims would do well to learn.
8. Have co-workers screen all calls and visitors.
9. Don't accept packages unless they were personally ordered.
10. Remove any name or identification from reserved parking at work.
11. Destroy discarded mail.
12. Equip your gas tank with a locking gas cap that can be unlocked only from inside the car.
13. Get a cell phone and keep it with you at all times, even inside your home, in case the stalker cuts your phone lines.
14. If you think you are being followed while in your car, make four left- or right-hand turns in succession. If the car continues to follow you, drive to the nearest police station - never home or to a friend's house.
15. Never be afraid to sound your car horn to attract attention.
16. Acquaint yourself with all-night stores and other public, highly populated places in your area.
17. Consider moving if your case warrants it. No, it's not fair – but nothing is fair about stalking. If you stay and fight through the legal system, you might get some justice (although not necessarily your definition of it) but you almost certainly won't get safety. There is no possibility of life imprisonment for stalkers. Research how to keep your destination secret. Stalking and victims' organisations can help.
18. Don't be embarrassed and think you caused this somehow. Stalkers need no encouragement. Your shame is your stalker's best weapon. It makes you more likely to engage him or agree to plea bargains,

which are bound to be taken as sympathy and we know where that leads. Instead, tell everyone you know that you're being stalked, from neighbours to co-workers, so that when the stalker approaches them for information about you, they will be alerted not to divulge anything and will let you know he's been around. One young widow moved to escape her stalker, a stranger she had never really met. Yet, after finding out where she moved, he was also able to pinpoint her exact location by showing her helpful neighbours; pictures he had surreptitiously taken of her and her children, telling them that he was her estranged husband and she had kidnapped the kids.

19. Join one of the stalking victims' support groups that are springing up all over the country. They can be invaluable resources for information in your community (such as how local law enforcement handles these cases) as well as provide essential support. If there is no group in your area, start one. It only takes two. Tragically, we can guarantee you are not the only person being stalked in your area.

Log on to www.antistalking.com website for information relating to:
- Restraining Orders,
- Stalker Violence;
- How to recognise a stalker;
- What to do/what not to do;
- Are you being stalked?
- Stalking behaviour Patterns and Cycles;
- Are there laws that make stalking a crime;
- Stalking Safety Plan Guidelines; and other relevant topics.

Another web site (www.obsessive-ex.com/oex) says ex partners suffer from what is called the Obsessive Ex Syndrome. These are people who are unable to mentally "let go" of a partner who leaves them.

Chapter 8
CHILD ABUSE

What is Child Abuse?

Abuse is defined in the dictionary as "an evil or corrupt practice; deceit, betrayal, molestation, violation" and comes in many forms. All abuse is violent, be it physical, emotional, psychological or a combination. The common denominator of all abuse is the collection of behaviours related to bullying. There are seven types of abuse:

Sexual - is the improper exposure of a child to sexual contact, activity or behaviour. It includes any sexual touching, intercourse or exploitation by anyone in whose care the child has been left or who takes advantage of a child. Such a person could be a parent, a relative, a friend or a stranger. Sexual abuse of a child is a criminal offence. It includes incest, rape, buggery or any paedophile activity for the gratification of the abuser. In cases of child abuse, the abuser usually has a sexually dysfunctional or unsatisfying relationship with his/her partner. Their sexual relations with their partner may be violent, inadequate or non-existent and the children may become convenient substitutes. Child abuse can begin when the mother is pregnant with another child and can't have sex.

Depending on its nature, its frequency and the child's relationship with the abuser, sexual abuse can have a variety of effects. The most serious are physical damage, feelings of betrayal, powerlessness, guilt, shame and confusion about sexuality and its expression. The increasing number of adults wanting counselling for childhood sexual abuse shows how long-lasting the effects of this type of child abuse are.

Physical - includes assault and any deliberate act resulting in physical injuries. This includes beating of children in the guise of corporal punishment - but which can be delivered with fists, through shaking or hits to the child's head. The intentional use of force on any part of a child's body that results in injuries is against the law. It may be a single incident or a series or pattern of incidents. The law states that physical force cannot be used on children unless the force used is "reasonable" and has been used for "corrective purposes" by a parent or someone acting in the role of parent.

Physical abuse can cause severe damage to children. That damage can be physical and/or psychological. It can take the form of permanent injury to a child's body as a result of broken bones, burns, shaking and being thrown about. Hearing can be damaged and mental functioning can be impaired.

Tactile - happens where there is little or no physical contact between parent(s) and the young child and any contact tends to be violent, punitive, unjust and inappropriate. Physical contact seems to be especially important in the first five or six years. Some children enjoy a cuddle into their teens. Sadly, with abuse coming into the open, many parents (especially fathers) now fear that physical contact with older children may be regarded and misconstrued as abuse.

Existence - where the existence and rights of the child are ignored through neglect of needs:

- Physical (food, clothing, shelter);
- Intellectual (education);
- Psychological (self-development, self-confidence, self-esteem, maturity);
- Behavioural (company, friendships, interpersonal and communication skills, relationships);
- Abandonment (leave child alone for long periods of time).
- Some ignore the child's existence or ignore one child and give love to others.

Religious or cult - The child is forced to accept the narrow, exclusive religious views of the parent or guardian to the exclusion of any other belief or possibility of any belief. Any behaviour by the child not in line with the parents' rigid religious zeal is met with punishment and abuse. The child is subjected to strange, unnatural and often perverse beliefs on sexual matters and sexual development in line with the religious belief. S/he is discouraged or prevented from associating with any person not sharing the religious belief of the parent or guardian. In some cases, the child may be subject to genital mutilation and as an adult are forced to live in isolation behind veils.

Emotional neglect - is the failure to meet the child's emotional needs for affection and a sense of belonging.

Emotional Abuse - is anything that causes serious mental or emotional harm to a child. Emotional abuse may take the form of verbal attacks on a child's sense of self, through repeated humiliation or rejection. Exposure to violence or severe conflict in the home, forced isolation, restraint or causing the child to be afraid much of the time, may also cause emotional harm. Emotional abuse rarely happens only once. It is usually part of a particular way of relating to children.

Parents who deliberately withhold love - are unwilling or have an inability to express love. Others give conditional love - that unless their children conform, they won't be loved. They love one child to the exclusion of others. They smother the child and deny the opportunity for him/her to develop as a separate individual. They force the child into conflict or use the children as a pawn between warring parents or witnessing violence between the parents. They place the child into a caretaker role at an inappropriate age. The child may be forced to witness alcohol or substance abuse or are forced to participate.

Emotional abuse affects a child's developing sense of self. Humiliation, rejection and insults can result in feelings of worthlessness and lack of confidence. It can cause general feelings of anxiety and insecurity that can affect every area of the child's life. The effects may show up as aggression, delayed development, depression or withdrawal. Children exposed to violence in their homes grow up with fear and insecurity. As well, they learn about the use of violence in close relationships and many grow up to repeat what they have learned.

Psychological - Parents give constant criticism or blame for trivial or unjustified reasons that may have no connection with the child. They refuse to acknowledge the child or their achievements and refuse to praise. Parents give unclear, shifting and inconsistent boundaries - sometimes no boundaries - and at other times give very tight boundaries. They use the silent treatment with the child. The child is exposed to the unpredictable behaviour of their parents. Psychologically, a child may feel unwanted, worthless and bad and may be violent with other people when s/he grows up.

Neglect - is any lack of care that causes serious harm to a child's development or endangers the child in any way. Neglect in its most extreme forms affects every part of a child's development. It can affect physical growth, mental development and emotional well-being.

Physical neglect - is the failure to meet the child's physical needs. This includes failing to provide adequate nutrition, clothing, shelter, health care and protection from harm.

Child abuse is anything that endangers the development, security or survival of a child. A child is anyone under the age of eighteen.

Smoke Gets in your Eyes - Excerpts from Elaine Hollingsworth's book Take Control of your Health and Escape the Sickness Industry
www.doctorsaredangerous.com

The most vulnerable passive smokers are babies in the womb. With every puff, the amount of blood and oxygen going to the foetus is decreased. This is what creates brain damage. Five minutes after the mother has a cigarette, her baby's heart speeds up and breathing movements decrease. These are signs of foetal distress. Blood pressure is raised during and after smoking. This is harmful to both mother and child. The mother's risk of having a stillborn baby is significantly increased and she is 80 percent more likely to have a spontaneous abortion than a non-smoker. If she smokes, her baby's body and brain will weigh less at birth and its chances of mental retardation and birth defects, such as port wine stain, cleft palate and harelip, will be higher.

There is strong evidence of development problems later in life and the child's height may be affected. Lower IQ scores, reading disability, behavioural problems and hyperactivity are all seen in the children of smoking mothers. Nothing can excuse a woman who allows such life-threatening things to happen to her unborn child!

Babies have small lungs and very small airways, so smoke-filled air impairs their breathing. Babies and young children breathe much faster than adults, meaning they inhale more air - and more pollution - in comparison to their body weight. Infants whose parents smoke at home have a higher rate of pneumonia and bronchitis. Many researchers have found that the dreaded sudden infant death syndrome is passive smoking-related. Zinc, which is vital for healthy growth in babies, becomes deficient in babies who are forced to breathe tobacco smoke. The breast milk of smoking women contains significant amounts of nicotine.

Second-hand smoke diminishes the blood supply to the bones and cuts off vital nutrients and contains up to 150 times higher levels of carcinogens than smoke directly inhaled by cigarette smokers. All smoking pollution remains long after the smoker has stopped. Even when a smoker inhales, researchers have calculated that two-thirds of the smoke from the burning cigarette goes into the environment. Insidiously, side-stream smoke contains far more of the carcinogenic tars and smoke particles and concentrations of noxious compounds than the mainstream smoke inhaled by the smoker. This exposure is deadly, because the toxic and carcinogenic chemicals released from the burning tip of the cigarette enter the atmosphere totally unfiltered by a mat of tobacco.

Some studies show there is twice as much tar and nicotine in side-stream smoke compared to main-stream; three times more of a compound called 3-4 benzopyrene, which is a carcinogen; five times more carbon monoxide, which robs the blood of oxygen; and 50 times more ammonia. There is also evidence that there is even more cadmium in side-stream smoke than in mainstream. Cadmium damages the air sacs of the lungs and causes emphysema. Once cadmium gets into your lungs, you've got it. It never goes away. 75 percent of the radiation in tobacco smoke enters the atmosphere and is inhaled by others. It is nothing short of criminal that smokers expose others [and especially their children] to additional, preventable doses of this deadly poison.

Doctors at the Royal Brisbane and Women's Hospital Research Foundation's Clinical Research Centre have found that smoking while pregnant blocks an adequate flow of iodine causing brain impairment in babies. Iodine is required to make thyroid hormone. Without iodine, the baby's brain doesn't develop as it should and results in lowered IQ levels. If babies don't have thyroid hormone, they can have very significant brain damage. Mothers who smoke ten to twenty cigarettes a day have enough thiocyanate in their blood to block the flow of iodine to their baby.

A shocking estimate is that twenty to thirty per cent of Australian women smoke during their pregnancies, affecting 76,500 babies born in Australia every year. To me, this is child abuse and the parents should be formally charged with the offence accordingly.

The Role of Society

In our society, we expect parents and guardians to care for their children in a loving and nurturing manner. Unfortunately there are some who are unable or unwilling to do this. Parents and teachers who cling to the myth that children are best left to resolve their own conflicts or if their children fight back just once, the bullying will stop or children who bully will just grow out of it - may inadvertently be adding to the problem.

Some reports suggest that one in four households is a site of violence. Since children are unable to care for themselves, others in the community must watch for incidents and situations that might be harmful to them. Children of all ages, from infancy to adolescence, from any kind of home and background, can be abused. Infants have been sexually abused and adolescents have been beaten and humiliated. Such children are described as "emotionally scarred". Many young people who run away from home are doing so to escape abusive situations.

It's difficult for these children to concentrate at school. When children have to sleep in the car because they have been locked out of the house by an abusive parent, it's impossible for them to finish their assignments or study for the next day's test. It's difficult for them to develop trusting relationships with their teachers and peers. If we want to do more than pay lip service to the needs of children, we must spend less time scape-goating mothers and allocate more resources to investigating and improving the lives of children who live with violence and fear.

Children learn violence from adults. Children learn to be victims from adults. Ask any shelter worker about three- and four-year old boys who abuse their mothers, demanding juice, calling them "Bitch," and kicking them in the shins if they don't react immediately. And the tiny girls who cringe when strangers speak to them. These children grow up to be abusers and victims and they repeat the cycle with their own children. Some become abusive parents themselves. A few become paedophiles and rapists, unable to distinguish between normal, loving sexual behaviour and the predatory behaviour they experienced as children. A tiny minority become murderous psychopaths. Most serial killers have a childhood history of violent physical and sexual abuse. The emotional scars from such experiences may run far deeper than we would like to believe.

Societal Passivity to Sexual Abuse at Home

In cases where a stranger commits child rape or abuse, society deals with it immediately and ruthlessly. But if a father, brother or mother commits the child rape or abuse, s/he rarely faces a jail term. If they receive a sentence, it's trivial when compared to stranger-child rape or abuse. This *must* change!

Physical and emotional child abuse is assault - and assault is a crime. Although most people in society would agree with this, somehow it remains deaf and dumb when it's faced with cases of incest. That assault not only destroys a childhood and removes sexual innocence, but sets the child up for a dysfunctional sexual future. These children have bruises on the inside and there are few laws in place to protect them.

The Role of Women in Child Abuse

Women who feel they must have a man at any price, often stand by and allow their children to be abused with the excuses:

a) *"That's the way I was treated when I was a child."* They use this as their excuse to pass bad feelings on to their children. They believe their actions can't be wrong, so absolve themselves of the responsibility and consequences of their actions. They do not have to pass on child abuse, but often if they don't receive professional help, that's exactly what happens.

b) *"He beats me too - I'm helpless."* Adults make a choice to stay in an abusive relationship - children don't have this choice unless society steps in.

c) *"Where was I supposed to go? I have no money."* Someone has to remove them, be it the other parent or society. That's what women's shelters are for.

d) *"My family turned their backs on me."* Blaming your family is refusing to accept the responsibility that you're an adult now. It's unlikely that your family will help you, if you too came from an abusive home.

Reporting Abuse

In younger children, maltreatment usually takes the form of physical abuse, in older children - neglect is more common. For child abuse to be reportable, parental behaviour must be inappropriate, dangerous and damaging. There is no law determining the age at which children can be left on their own, but authorities can remove youngsters if their safety is at risk. Parents who leave children in dangerous situations can be charged and the age of the child is immaterial. Parents need to consider not only the age but the state of their child's development.

We live in a society where other people care for children. The most common injury that's seen is bruises. Other signs of abuse include injuries in regular patterns, lacerations in unusual places, genital tears, burns, fractures of all kinds and head injuries. In most cases of abuse, the abuser inflicts the injuries using something within easy reach such as a belt or electrical cord. Hot water burns caused by placing a child in scalding hot water are among the common injuries.

Sexual abuse has ramifications for life. Children who are sexually abused have the whole fabric of their life changed. If daddy has sex with them every Wednesday night while mommy goes to bingo, for four years of their lives, it changes who they are and what they become. The definition of child sexual abuse is a child used as an object for the sexual gratification of the adult.

Then there's Munchausen where the parent receives reflected attention by making the child sick.

Government Social Services departments have the legal responsibility to investigate all reported cases of suspected child abuse and take appropriate action. Some practices, which we once considered acceptable, are now believed to be abusive. If physical or sexual assaults are suspected, reports should be made to the police.

Why does child abuse happen?

The abuse of children is a very complicated issue. There are many factors that contribute to it.

- Some parents believe it is their right and duty to control their children and to use whatever means they think are required to do so.
- Other parents are abusive because they are unwilling to care for their children properly. The children are unwanted or are a nuisance to them. They find their children too much of a burden. Such unwilling parents usually think that their own needs are more important than their children's.
- In the case of sexual abuse, some abusers believe that they have the right to have their sexual and/or intimacy needs met by the children they are abusing.
- Some parents abuse their children because, having grown up in abusive families, they have not learned to raise children in any other way.
- Some children are abused because their parents do not understand child development and therefore do not know how to meet their children's needs. They may have unrealistic expectations of the

children and punish them when they do not meet those expectations.
- Some children are abused because their parents have too few resources. They may not have enough time, energy, money and/or support to care for their children properly. Too much stress may contribute to abuse.

How can you identify child abuse?

The following indicators may help alert you to the possibility of abuse:

- Unexplained bruises, welts or injuries, especially in places that children do not normally injure during regular play or movement.
- Burns that leave a pattern outlining the object which was used to make the burn, such as a cigarette, an iron or an electric stove burner; burns on the hands, feet or buttocks caused by scalding water or rope burns caused by being tied.
- A child who is continually hungry, unsuitably dressed for the weather and/or always dirty.
- A young child who is often left alone.
- A child who is unusually aggressive, angry and hostile with other people.
- A child who demonstrates withdrawal behaviour, who refuses to participant or dress appropriately for physical activities.
- A child who shows unusual knowledge of sexual matters, who acts sexually provocative around adults or who shows unusual fear of a particular adult, adults of a particular sex or adults in general.
- A child who hints or talks about sexual abuse.

Domestic violence and children

In homes where domestic violence occurs, children are also at high risk of suffering physical, sexual and emotional abuse. Whether or not they are physically abused, children who witness domestic violence suffer significant emotional and psychological trauma said to be similar to that experienced by victims of child abuse.

Research confirms that abusive men often escalate violence to re-capture their partner and children who have sought safety in separation. The risk to children in the context of domestic violence separation is substantial. Yet the risk is virtually invisible.

Dealing with Domestic Violence and Child Abuse

While the impact of domestic violence on women has "come out of the closet" over the course of the last twenty years, the impact and risk of domestic violence for children remains a closely held secret.

Women's shelters recognise that a child living in an environment where domestic violence occurs is an abused child. Not all children are affected by domestic violence in the same way. It can impact on every aspect of a child's life and behaviour.

Reactions of children exposed to domestic violence:

- Isolation:
- Feeling responsible for the abuse;
- Helplessness;
- Guilt for not stopping the abuse;
- Medical problems;
- Grief;
- Ambivalence;
- Fear of abandonment;
- Embarrassment;
- Pessimism about the future;
- Eating and sleeping disorders;
- Depression;
- Detachment;
- Fantasies about normal life.

Reactions of adolescents to domestic violence

- Poor grades, school drop-out;
- Low self-esteem;
- Refusal to bring friends home - stays away;
- Runs away;
- Isolated;
- Violent outbursts;
- Irresponsible decision-making;
- Eating disorders;
- Run away;
- Suicide attempts;
- Substance abuse and other delinquent behaviours;
- Unable to communicate feelings;
- Nightmares;

- Depression;
- Dating violence;
- Physical symptoms;
- A temptation to fight back no matter what the consequences

When children are brought up under those constant conditions the areas of the brain, which control their interpersonal, behavioural and social skills fail to develop normally. The violence and sexual abuse in infancy and childhood can cause permanent changes to the structure and wiring of the brain that psychotherapy and drugs may not be able to repair. Childhood abuse within the critical time when the brain is being physically sculpted by experience imposes severe stress that can disrupt its structure and function. Later in life these changes can cause depression, anxiety, suicidal thoughts and post-traumatic stress disorder. The children express their mental state through aggression, impulsiveness, delinquency, hyperactivity or drug abuse.

Borderline Personality Disorder (BPD) is strongly associated with ill treatment in early childhood. People with BPD tend to see others in black-and-white terms - almost worshipping them at one moment, then vilifying them for some perceived slight. They have almost volcanic outbursts of anger.

These damaged children lack the ability to control frustration or anger or to monitor or control violent behaviour. They take no responsibility or understood the consequences of their actions and show little or no concern for others. In many cases of violent offenders, their brain's ventral region of the frontal lobes - which modify and control violent rages, are measurably smaller than in normal people.

The key to successful treatment is to act as quickly as possible while the developing brain was most capable of adapting to change. Magnetic resonance imaging (MRI) is a powerful tool for examining brains. Several MRI studies have shown that, in abuse victims, the hippocampus is reduced in volume by an average of 12 per cent and seemed to involve only the left side. If some key function is damaged in childhood, it's well established that other parts of a child's brain can be developed to pick up such functions. Rigorous training in interpersonal and social skills and establishing rules of conduct would encourage other parts of the brain to acquire that control. In the future, genetic intervention to curb anti-social behaviour may be a possibility.

Children who have known no other way of life, may think their abusive environment is normal. They may blame themselves, believing that they have done something to deserve the abuse. Some abused children grow up to repeat the abusive child-rearing style of their parents. Others are fearful that they will be abusive parents and may refuse to have children for that reason.

Children are wholly dependent on their parent(s) and the parent(s) possess, in the eyes of their children, a God-like status. In the eyes of the child, his/her parents can do no wrong and become his/her role models. Therefore, when a child is smacked - s/he doesn't know it's not the way his/her behaviour should be corrected. S/he may feel that, *"I'm bad, so I'm therefore being justly punished."* No person can ever be bad; it's their behaviour that's bad. The lesson that it teaches is that violence is an acceptable solution to problems.

For many, relief from their pain - or their memory of pain from corporal punishment, can only be obtained by doing the same to others. This is known as displacement aggression. He hit me and I can't hit him back, so instead I'll hit somebody else. The child who is subjected to regular abuse needs an outlet for his/her aggression and may act out violent impulses on another child at school, a sibling or a family pet. Violence towards animals such as torturing a cat or killing a dog is now recognised as a common early warning sign of forthcoming violence in adulthood.

A Safety Plan for Children

It's very important for children who live in violent homes to have a simple safety plan:

- Warn children to stay out of the adult conflicts.
- Make a list of people the children can trust and talk to when they are feeling unsafe (neighbours, teachers, relatives, friends).
- Decide ahead of time on a safe place the children can go when they feel unsafe.
- Teach children how to use police and other emergency phone numbers.

Often when children are removed from a situation where violence is occurring along with their mothers and they are supported with specialist help, the behavioural and emotional effects of domestic violence will improve. Psychologists insist potential danger signs are readily identifiable.

Apart from the emotional, physical, social and behavioural damage abuse creates for children; statistics show that domestic violence can also become a learned behaviour. This means that children may grow up to think it is okay to use violence to get what they want and that as adults, it is okay for there to be violence in their relationships.

Australian children at risk

An Australian study shows that almost 20,000 Australian children were on care and protection court orders and placed with relatives, in foster or residential care in 2000 - 01. Unfortunately, the perpetrator of the abuse was most frequently a natural parent. The number of indigenous children on care and protection orders was six times the rate of other Australian children. It found a high proportion of abused children were found to come from female-headed, one-parent families.

Federal Minister for Children, Larry Anthony said the report highlighted a need for uniform child protection laws across states and territories. These laws need minimum standards for mandatory reporting and for the investigation of child abuse and neglect allegations.

The study also found that more girls than boys were subject to abuse and neglect and that three times as many girls as boys were subject to sexual abuse.

Victoria's child welfare system is in crisis, with record numbers of young children being abused. The State Government has set up a high-level taskforce to tackle the problem. Figures released by Community Services Minister Bronwyn Pile reveal that:

- 36,799 cases of suspected child abuse cases were reported last year;
- Department of Human Services officers substantiated 7,608 cases where children were bashed sexually and emotionally abused or neglected;
- 591 children were sexually abused;
- 1,988 were physically abused;
- 1,745 were neglected;
- 3,284 were emotionally abused;
- 59 per cent of victims were under nine years of age;
- 37 per cent of victims were from single parent families;
- 3,882 children were placed in out-of-home care;

- About 88 per cent of children in care were removed from their homes by court orders.

Ms Pike commented, *"Not only do we have to put resources into the child protection system, but we have to look at systemic reform and how we can most effectively use our resources."* She added, *"We want to identify families at risk and bring them into the family and child health system, make sure young people are participating in schools and strengthen family support, education and foster care."*

Opposition Community Services spokes woman Lorraine Elliott said, *"We need to identify at risk children at birth and constantly monitor those families. The Government has to establish a central register of at risk children that can be accessed by professionals."*

A Picture of Australia's Children - The Australian Institute of Health and Welfare - assisted by funding from the Australian Government Department of Health and Ageing.

In Australia, child protection is the responsibility of the state and territory governments. The AIHW has played a leading role in the monitoring and reporting of children's services, child protection and children's health and wellbeing since 1996. Their report includes information about individual, family and societal factors that influence the health and wellbeing of children. Topics include exposure to environmental tobacco smoke, homelessness, literacy and numeracy, children as victims of violence, neighbourhood safety and parental health and disability. Excerpts from the report state:

- There were approximately 3.9 million children aged 0-14 years in Australia in 2003.
- The rate of children in care and protection orders increased by 47% between 1997 and 2003. However this increase needs to be interpreted with caution as the trends in such data are heavily influenced by changes in policies and practices within the child protection system.
- The rate of children who were placed in out-of home care rose from 3 per 1,000 children in 1997 to 5 per 1,000 in 2004.
- On average, 25 Australian children are killed by their parents each year (Mouzos & Rushforth 2003).
- Over 12,000 victims of all types of assault were recorded by police in 2003.

- Boys aged 10-14 years (800 per 100,000 children) were assaulted more than any other group of children. Boys were assaulted at higher rates than females in both age groups.
- Rates of rep\orted sexual assault against girls aged 10-14 years were higher than those recorded for boys. Rates of sexual assault among these girls were five times those recorded for boys (475 compared with 88 per 100,000). Girls aged 10-14 years were sexually assaulted at twice the rate of girls aged 0-9 years. The rate of sexual assaults for boys was similar for both age groups and was consistently lower than the rate for girls.

Victims of assault and sexual assaults not only experience harm in the short-term, but are at risk of further harm or harming others later in life. Find more information on their website: www.aihw.gov.au/publications

Behavioural Problems

Some children who live with violence become aggressive. Uncontrollable anger is a common outlet for feelings that are otherwise difficult to express. For some, there is a tendency to never be seen as weak or needing help from anyone. Angry children are very good at hiding their need for love and security.

Other children show opposite behaviour and become withdrawn and fearful. Direct attacks from their parent's anger are often handled by running or hiding, shocked silence and clinging. These children can be very passive and easily withdrawn. Children and teenagers from violent homes may become depressed and the risk of suicide cannot be ignored.

Children who learn to accept violence and aggression as normal in their families often avoid forming close relationships with others. The message they get from their parents is twofold. Firstly, relationships are seen as being based on manipulation and submission rather than love and mutual trust; secondly, those whom you love and trust hurt you the most.

Children often blame themselves for the abuse they witness in their families. Some experience guilt, feeling they should have endured the punishment rather than their mother. It is common for these children to seek punishment through other behaviours such as lying, stealing and throwing temper tantrums.

Children who witness or experience abuse may also have problems dealing with authority. Running away from home and failing in school are two examples of problems related to dealing with authority.

Counsellors and therapists who work with children who have behavioural problems now recognise that many of these problems are directly related to living in violent homes.

Fathers renege financial responsibilities

Children are disadvantaged by only having a single parent at home. Not because of the missing parent - but because women and children of broken homes are often forced to live in poverty.

Jake Najman, Director of the Queensland Alcohol and Drug Research and Education Centre, said, *"While it was true children from single-parent families had increased risks of mental and other health problems, this was tied more to poverty than it was to the single-mother status. We know that children coming from impoverished families have higher rates of drug dependency and they have higher rates of suicide. It's higher because they are economically disadvantaged, but it doesn't mean it's higher because of single mothers. Many northern European countries realise the implications poverty held for children's health and had begun to help mothers to go back to work and to complete their educations to better the family's economic circumstances."*

Paedophiles

Parents who say, *"Of course I'd know if my child was being abused. I've taught my children to come straight to me if something like that ever happened to them"* shouldn't be so complacent. Child molesters make it their business to operate without detection. They engage in behaviours designed to make it difficult for a child to resist reporting the abuse and even harder for a child to disclose. For decades parents bought the comforting myth of the dirty old man in the brown coat offering candy. This lingering stereotype allowed many abusers to prey on children without arousing suspicion.

The paedophile creates many victims. An American study of the Emery University concluded that 403 paedophiles had made 67,000 victims together; with an average of 166 victims per person! After the death of Australian Clarence Osborn, a lot of photographs, notes and tapes were found. They bore witness to the 2,500 small boys he had sex with.

More than ten million children are sexually abused by adults worldwide and the number of victims of child prostitution, child rape and child pornography is increasing. Every year more than a million new children are being kidnapped, bought or forced to take part in the sex-market in one way or another. The children are getting younger and younger. As a consequence, more and more children are being infected with Aids.

Most grownups are nice to children and care about what happens to them. But every now and then there are grown-ups who touch children in a way that's not okay. This could be a person they know and trust, such as a teacher, a relative or a neighbour.

The majority of abusers are male and they may be of any age. Paedophilia is a lifelong compulsive condition that often emerges when the child is in adolescence. Children are far more likely to be abused by a male who is well known to them or their family.

If the abuser is not a family member, he will usually be someone the parents trust and accept. The abused child is aware of the warm relationship between his/her parents(s) and his/her molester. For the child, this adult association makes sexual abuse even more difficult to disclose.

What do these abusers look for in their victims? While some abuse is unplanned, most abusers actively seek out children who appear lonely, needy and less likely to tell others about the abuse. Children with unfulfilled needs for affection and attention are the most vulnerable. Hungry for love, they rapidly bond with a "loving" abuser and develop an inappropriate sense of loyalty to their abusers.

Abusers count on this close bond with the child to continue their abuse. They purchase their acceptance and silence by giving affection and attention (gifts, surprises and special outings). During the initial stages, they test the child's resistance towards advancing their sexual intimacy with them.

The emotional bond allows the molestation to continue and at the same time makes the abuse more difficult for the child to report to others.

Abusers obtain excitement and satisfaction from the ritual of finding and preparing a child for their abuse. Emotional and physical preparation may go on for months before the actual sexual touching starts. The child becomes used to being touched by the abuser in an affectionate way, which is often done in front of the child's parents.

This might be through roughhousing; giving hugs and kisses, sitting on their lap or occasional touching during games.

Overt sexual touching often takes the child by surprise. The child may not initially object, because the shift from playful and affectionate to erotic touch may be too subtle.

Abusers use this perceived "co-operation" to rationalise this abusive behaviour. They believe that the child wants the contact because there was no resistance to it. In fact, the child is often unaware for some time of what is actually happening. Once the child realises what the behaviour actually is, they may be reluctant to tell others out of fear of punishment for their "participation."

Abusers convince themselves that they are not harming these children, but "teaching" them the secrets of love and sex. This preposterous notion is strongly supported if the child physically responds to their sexual touch. Their bodies are hot-wired for erotic responses from birth, so they have little control over their responses. Should a boy gets an erection during abuse or a girl feels pleasure, not only does the abuser feel his irrational thinking is justified, but the child's ability to self-protect itself from further incidents is damaged by the guilt they feel for feeling that pleasure.

We tell children that abuse feels yucky. Violation usually ends up feeling awful, but may not necessarily start out that way. Abusers admit that they target families where they are likely to gain private access to children. This may be achieved through seemingly harmless activities such as babysitting, helping with homework, holidays, outings, camping or sleepovers.

One ticket of entry is to romance a single mom and take on the surrogate father role. Another is to become the friendly "uncle" to the kids.

Abusers become experts at spotting and exploiting dysfunctional family units.

They understand that the child with difficult behaviour can be manipulated far easier than the child who has a good relationship with his/her parents.

So how can we keep our children safe? We can talk to our children about good and bad touching, give proper names to body parts and sexual activities and the importance of telling if they aren't comfortable when others touch them.

Any adult who becomes emotionally important to a child is in a position to take advantage of that relationship. We wrongly assume that an adult's interest must be innocent. Sadly, the stronger the interest, the more we need to suspect abuse.

While there is no definable way to abuse-proof children, we can minimise the risks by giving our children adequate love, time, affection and attention, so they don't look for it elsewhere.

Paedophiles in the workplace

Canadian courts have ruled that employers will be held vicariously liable where employees have engaged in illegal or negligent conduct during their employment. This includes adults who are in positions of trust for the care of children. The need for employers to engage in effective management practices has been reflected in a Canadian Supreme Court decision.

For instance, a paedophile was hired as a supervisor by a foundation that operated as a home for troubled children. The foundation did not know the employee was a paedophile. When they checked before an offer of employment was made, they were told he was a suitable employee. During the course of his workplace duties, the employee sexually assaulted one of the children. As soon as this was known, the foundation immediately discharged him.

The courts found the employer vicariously liable for the employee's conduct. Although the employer was not found negligent, the court found that vicarious liability arises where the employer's business creates or enhances a risk and where there is a significant connection between that risk and the employee's wrongful act.

The court also listed several factors that could be considered when dealing with vicarious liability:

- The amount of power given to an employee in relation to the victim.
- The level of vulnerability of victims to the wrongful exercise of the employee's power
- The chance the venture gave to employees to abuse their power.
- The extent to which the wrongful act furthered the aims of the employer.

The imposition of vicarious liability has been deemed necessary to provide fair compensation for wrongdoings and to deter future wrongs. As a result, a higher degree of supervision and care needs to be exercised by employers - especially those in service industries dealing with children. Employers need to set strict standards of permissible and impermissible behaviour and give training to ensure their employees understand their policies and the consequences of breaching those policies.

In Australia, a screening system for people who work with youngsters, the elderly and the disabled ensures that people working with these groups have qualified for a "Blue Card." To obtain a "Blue Card" they must pass rigid police checks to ensure they are suitable people to work with these often defenseless people..

It also includes a check on apprehended violence orders and disciplinary proceedings. The legislation applies to people working in schools and preschools, childcare centres, hospitals, refuges, religious organisations, clubs and associations with significant child/elderly/disabled membership. It includes ministers of religion and foster carers.

Advice For Children: (A talk adults can give to children)

Everyone likes to be hugged or touched by someone they care for. But there are some kinds of touching that are not considered good for kids. Some of this kind of touching might feel good. Some of this kind of touching might feel bad or even hurt. If you aren't sure about a touch, talk to a trusted adult about it. Most adults care about kids and never sexually abuse them. But some people have serious problems and think it's okay to be sexual with a child. Sometimes a sexual abuser is a stranger, but usually a sexual abuser would be someone you know. It might be your parent or stepparent, neighbour, minister or a friend of your parents. It might be a relative such as an uncle or cousin or someone that you like a lot. Someone who sexually abuses a child has a problem and needs help. People can do bad things - even nice people. It's sometimes hard to believe that someone we love or who is nice to us can sexually abuse us.

Some children blame themselves, but they shouldn't. Adults sometimes use tricks like telling them that they are bad and that this is why this happened. Also, the attention can sometimes seem nice. This person may give you gifts or money when s/he wants to touch you. Whether his/her touch is violent or gentle - it is very, very wrong and must be stopped. No matter what, if you are being sexually abused, it is never your fault. You need to:

Keep telling until someone listens. Some adults do not know what to do when a young person tells them about sexual abuse. An adult may tell them not to talk about it or to forget it. They may even accuse you of making up stories. You should not give up and find someone to tell who will help you.

Remember, adults and older kids should never:

- Ask you to keep a secret about touching;
- Touch you anywhere that is private, like where your bathing suit covers you;
- Ask you to touch them anywhere private;
- Reach under your clothes or try to get you to take off your clothes;
- Ask you to keep a secret about something wrong;
- Try to take pictures of you without your clothes;
- Ask you to touch yourself or other kids anywhere private.

For Parents:

The most important sexual abuse prevention strategy is good communication with your child. Take the time every day to talk with your child and make sure that you really listen and observe while s/he talks. Encourage your child to share his or her problems and concerns with you. Talk to your child about sexual abuse. Use the proper words for sex organs, such as penis and vagina. It is hard for a child to talk openly about sexual abuse if s/he doesn't have the words or has been taught that parts of the body are dirty or bad. If your child says s/he doesn't like someone or shows reluctance or discomfort around an adult or teenager, ask why. Ask if the person has done something to make him or her feel uncomfortable. A sexually abused child may show unusual interest in sexuality.

Here are a few things you can tell children that can help them if it ever happens to them:

Their body belongs to them.

No one has the right to touch them if they don't want them to. This includes uncles and aunts, mom, dad, teachers, coaches and grandparents - everyone.

- There are places on their body that are private - like places your swimming suit covers that adults should not try to touch (unless it's their doctor and their parent or guardian is in the room with them).
- They need to trust their feelings. If something feels wrong, they should object. It is all right to say *"No"* to an adult who tries to do something that's wrong.
- They should tell someone they trust about what has happened - even if the person said it was a secret or that they would hurt you or someone else if they told about the incident.
- If someone does something to them that is wrong, they may tell them it's a special secret or make them promise not to tell. Explain that it's okay to break this kind of promise - the person who made them promise - knows that they were doing something very wrong.

If your child becomes a victim of sexual abuse

Many children who tell adults about crimes are afraid they will not be believed. Many aren't. Be sure to take your child seriously, even if a violent crime has not been committed. Reassure the child that what happened is not his or her fault. A child who was hurt or accosted while breaking a rule (such as being somewhere you said they were not allowed to go) may be especially afraid that you will be upset with him or her.

Immediately get the child to medical attention. In the case of sexual assault, an injury might not be obvious and a medical examination is required to detect internal injuries and screen for possible exposure to disease or infection.

Try to control your own reaction. Your child is likely to become very upset if s/he sees that you are upset. S/he may also think that s/he did something wrong and take responsibility for your pain. S/he may decide it is better not to keep talking to you if you exhibit extreme emotions.

Report the crime - even a suspected crime - to the police. Don't try to take the law into your hands. Your child needs you and needs to try to get back some normalcy in his or her life. If you try to harm someone who has hurt your child, you could be arrested and even go to jail. Your child would then have to cope with that added trauma.

Chapter 9
CASE STUDIES - CHILD ABUSE

18 month-old twins starved to death

June 16, 2008, Sunnybank Hills, Queensland – The 11-year-old sister of 18-month-old twins (a boy and a girl) found their corpses after they had lain in their cots dead for more than a week. They allegedly died of malnutrition. The sister had found the corpses after smelling a foul odour coming from behind the door. She allegedly told her 30-year-old mother: *"I know why you've been crying now."* The twins' short lives were even a mystery to their elder brothers and sister, who rarely saw them outside the room.

"I don't think I fed them enough," the mother of six allegedly told officers when asked why her children had died. Police allege the twins - hidden from the outside world - were slowly starved to death. By the time the tiny bodies of the boy and girl were found they weighed just 3.6kg and 4kg - about the same as a newborn baby. The couple were charged with two counts each of failing to supply the necessities of life dating back to October 1, 2007.

Neighbours said they had not heard or seen anything to indicate something was amiss. Most of the neighbours did not even know about the existence of the twins. The only clues to their existence were a twin stroller and the little pink and blue clothes on the washing line in a backyard strewn with toys. Police, alerted by a relative, arrived at the modest brick home about 7 pm to find a gruesome scene in a front bedroom.

The court was told the father, a 28-year-old project manager, who lived in the house but was estranged from the mother, had not seen the children for about six months.

There were also some reports that some of the older children were not attending school. A neighbour says older children from the family often came over looking for food. A neighbour said she had lived in the same street as the family for five years and sometimes gave food to the children in the family.

"The youngest boy (a four-year-old boy) came over here and said, `I need something to eat, I'm hungry,'" the neighbour said. *"When they*

came here about four months ago I give them some snacks or fruit with my children but after that I stopped it."

"I never see the mother or the father also, I just see the kids because they come around my house," she said.

"Sometimes you would hear her yelling at the kids, but it wasn't abusive," neighbour Mehmet Ozkan said. *"And what parent doesn't yell at their kids now and then."*

Mr. Ozkan said it did worry him that a little boy - aged about three or four years - would wander into his yard and hang around for some time. *"I thought it was a bit strange he was left on his own like that. You hardly ever saw the parents,"* he said.

The twins' sister, 11 and three brothers, aged 3, 4 and 5 are now in the care of their maternal grandmother. She said they were healthy but too young to comprehend what had happened. Her grandchildren were *"very traumatised,"* she said. *"We are doing the best we can for them, just to know they are wanted and loved."*

The father 28 and his partner, who cannot be named for legal reasons, were charged with failing to provide the necessities of life. They were remanded in custody after police prosecutor Sgt. Tina Clark asked that both be kept behind bars for 48 hours to await the results of autopsies which would decide if further charges were laid. The woman and her estranged partner had initially been charged with neglect, but were later charged with murder and torture.

Child sexual abuse cases

Three tragic cases of child abuse happened within one week in Queensland and are likely just the tip of the iceberg. Queensland Families Minister Judy Spence stated that none of these cases had been reported to welfare for investigation. One involved an 18-month-old child, Beanca Newman, who had been bound hand and foot and 'hogtied' by her parents in a futile effort to make her sleep in her own bed. She had thrashed and turned in distress and screamed until she fell asleep until one morning she did not wake up. Her parents, Daniel Green, 25 and Rebecca Haliday, 22, were charged with manslaughter.

Two other abused children died as well. Three-year-old Tyler Newman died after being punched, beaten and kicked by his stepfather and nine-month-old Madisen Abigail Fahy died from a head wound and massive internal injuries.

Field workers relate an increase in abuse and neglect is a result of increasing drug use and disintegration of family units. The trend is leaning towards early intervention to break the cycle of abuse. In October 2002, Spence announced a 12-month trial of 31 new prevention and early intervention services in Queensland costing $15.8 million.

Denise was eleven and her breasts were beginning to grow. Her uncle started "accidentally" touching her breasts every chance he got. Later on, he would go into her bedroom and reach under the sheets and touch her breasts. Denise pretended to be asleep and did not move when he molested her.

Hector was ten and loved playing soccer. His coach gave him a lot of attention and would give him rides after practice. The coach told Hector that there was a special game they could play. The game was fun except for the part where the coach had Hector hold and touch his penis. Hector wanted to stop, but the coach said if he did, then he wouldn't get to play soccer any more so he was forced to allow his coach to continue abusing him.

Jenny was seven. She liked her mother's boyfriend because he always wanted her to dance with him, but he would kiss her and rub his body up against her and reach up under her dress when her mom was away. He said it was their special secret. This is how many paedophiles obtain access to vulnerable children – by dating their single Moms.

Tyrone was fourteen. A 25-year-old friend of his sister wanted to take Tyrone's picture. Tyrone thought it would be fun. Because it was a hot day, the photographer asked Tyrone to take off his shirt. Then she told Tyrone to take off his pants, like he was in an underwear commercial. When she told Tyrone to take off his underwear, he said no, but she told him that if he didn't she would show everyone the pictures of him in his underwear. So he did as she asked and she took photos of him in the nude.

Sarah was eleven and her stepfather was sexually abusing her. He said that Sarah's mom didn't love him, so he wanted Sarah to be his girlfriend. The abuse had worsened the last few months, but Sarah was too afraid to tell. Her stepfather said her mom would be hurt if Sarah told anyone. When her stepfather had sex with her, Sarah felt like she wanted to die.

Abusive parents hide behind legal loophole:

Almost 700 Queensland parents a year are charged with assaulting their children – but many get off because they can legally claim they were using "reasonable force" to discipline them (Section 280 of the Criminal Code). Of those, 14 were grievous assaults and 388 were serious assaults. These shocking figures have been released by the Queensland State Government and prompted former state attorney-general and minister for justice, Dean Wells to call for a change to the Criminal Code that protects parents.

The Labor Member for Murrumba said there was a need for reform of this "archaic and dangerous" section of the Criminal Code. *"This section, which says it is lawful for a parent or person in place of a parent to use reasonable force for the purposes of the correction or discipline of a child, legitimates more violence than any child deserves to have brought against them,"* he said. This Section 280 defence had been used in court in cases where a parent threatened a child with a knife, threw a child into a door frame or punched a child in the chest for bed-wetting. In New Zealand the parents were acquitted despite using horsewhips on a 12-year-old girl and blocks of wood were used to discipline their children.

Women's Safety, Women's Voices - Office of Women's Policy, Department for Victorian community.

Julie

"I was sexually abused by my uncle, who was my father's sister's husband, when I was about nine. I didn't know him very well. I grew up overseas and we didn't come to Australia until I was eight and it was about six months after that it happened," she said.

"I had only known him for a few months but it was nevertheless a betrayal of trust because you trust adults. The night it happened, I told my mother and was in quite a state. She believed me and at the time I told her not to tell anybody because I was so ashamed and embarrassed. She told my dad and he rang his sister straight away and told her what had happened. When she confronted her husband, he told her that we were playing doctors and nurses, which is what he had told me to say if anyone asked what we were doing. My parents were very avoidant types and I hadn't been actually raped. They didn't know what to do so nothing was done.

"When the perpetrator is a family member, it's difficult to address. My father had mixed loyalties. He felt for his sister. Some of the family believed me and some didn't. My other uncle and aunt believed me, but the perpetrator's wife didn't believe me and "He said, 'No to all your questions' and said that he would go to counselling if that would make me happy. He said that he was sorry I felt it had affected my life like this, that it was all a gross misunderstanding and that he wished that it could have been sorted out at the time with a little discussion."

The results for Julie were dramatic. She said her aunt rang her and said, 'What the hell have you done? He gave you all he could in the letter. You've just blown things up way too far. He's gone to England and he's left us a suicide note.' Another unsigned letter arrived from her uncle denying everything and saying 'By the time you get this, I'll be gone'.

Julie's decision to confront her uncle caused real problems between her and her family. "From then on", she said, *"my parents got involved. Dad rang up and said, 'What have you done? Things are way out of proportion and it ends here'. My mum said that I was oversensitive and that I just couldn't let things lie.'*

"All I wanted was for them to understand and I argued and fought and cried, but it didn't make any different. Counselling groups helped me come to terms with a few things. I know that Mum and Dad just can't look at it and they can't deal with it. I am not going to get what I want."

Julie said that if this happened to her child she would get the child some counselling and confront the perpetrator straight away, make them take some action to address their problem and make them apologise to the child. "It's not up to the child to confront this big scary person. At the end of the day, an adult can look after themselves, but a child can't - they need you." *Julie said.*

neither did my grandparents. I was once talking to my Grandmother as an adult and she said, 'But wasn't he drunk or something? Wasn't it something that you just got wrong?' It seemed as if it just upset the whole family and so my parents decided that they wouldn't talk about it again and they hoped that I would just forget it.

"My parents stopped inviting that uncle and his wife to our house, but at family functions he would be there, staring at me all the time. I hated being put in that position and my parents just didn't seem to notice his staring. When I got older, when I was a teenager, I would ask them,

'Can we leave?' They would say, *'Yes, yes, soon.'* I remember once I walked out and walked home in tears by myself. I used to have nightmares about my uncle trying to get in the door while I was trying to hold the door shut. I grew up not trusting men and disrespecting them too. In my teen years I was sometimes suicidal.

"It hurt me that after a few years my parents started to talk to him. It felt like they just didn't care what he had done to me. I would talk to my mother and she would say, 'God doles out punishment in his own way and in his own time.'

"When I was about 20, I heard about a girl who used to be my uncle's neighbour. She was a similar age to me. I was told that my uncle had done it to her too. I was angry. If something had been done at the time of either incident, then at least one of us would have been saved from having that pain.

"One of the biggest problems I have had is this 'forgive and forget.' If you can't forgive and forget you are made to feel like a terrible person, that you're not doing the right thing. It's all a lot of rot. You don't need to forgive, you need to let go, but that's different. It can happen only after validation. It takes time and support.

"I saw a counsellor and brought up my childhood experiences and was asked if I wanted to confront him in any way to let him know how it made me feel and how it affected me. I said 'Yes.' I didn't want to take it to court. I know the success rate is not very high. I know the way they treat you and didn't want to put my family through that. But I did want him to know that what he had done was a crime."

Julie wrote her uncle a letter. In the letter she asked him why he did what he did, whether he had ever been abused himself, whether he had ever done it to anyone else and whether he would consider going to counselling. She also said that she would like a reply and that if she didn't get a reasonable response, she would consider taking it to court. The reply Julie received did not satisfy her.

Case Study - Monster Dad

My mother was married for eighteen years to a monster we called "dad." She thought we were safe because he didn't rip off our clothes, threaten us with a gun, choke, kick, stab, punch, shove or scream at us. But she was wrong. She didn't realise that he didn't need to do any of those things because we were already paralysed with fear from what he did to our mother. I was scared because my mother was scared.

Many times, my mother took us to spend the night with relatives or friends, but we always went back. I couldn't concentrate in school and my grades were terrible. I tried to be like the other kids, but the teachers labelled me lazy and stupid. The only lesson I learned was that I shouldn't count on anyone to help me; that I was on my own.

I'm not a psychologist, but I know what I have lived through and who I am. I seem like everyone else. I smile and am friendly, but no one, not even my family members, can get close to me. I know deep down that my underlying hostility and distrust of people is crippling and has prevented me from developing close relationships.

To spare other young lives this unhealthy, lonely existence, I beg all battered women - if you don't care about yourself - please care about your children and get out now!

Case Study - Janet

Janet knew that her children's stepfather was sexually abusing them, but chose to remain silent rather than face his wrath. She said, *"I was too embarrassed to say anything and let everyone know what was going on in our family."* She allowed her "embarrassment" of others finding out overshadow her responsibility as a mother to do something about the situation. How could Janet be "too embarrassed" to protect her children from her abusive husband who was ruining their young lives?

Those who grow up in homes devoid of abuse, realise that the mother was as guilty as her husband, because she did nothing to end the abuse. In fact, her lack of positive action made it possible for that abuse to go on year after year. Many believe that she too should be charged with child abuse because she failed to protect them when she knew they were being abused.

Unfortunately, Janet had no inclination that hers was anything but a normal household. She was eleven the first time she had been sexually abused. First it was her father, then later her brother who copied his father's unacceptable behaviour. This cycle goes on and on. If that family looked back two or three generations, they'd probably find that this was typical familial behaviour.

Case Study - Debra

After a life of abuse at the hands of her father and a troubled twelve-year marriage, Debra Williams-Poppe had found happiness with a new man. She and her husband celebrated their second wedding anniversary only days before her father lured her to his bungalow and shot her dead before turning the gun on himself. Only days before he killed his daughter, Williams was released from a hospital mental ward where he was a frequent patient. Bill Williams blamed his daughter for the break-up of his own marriage. Williams' wife had recently suffered two heart attacks and made the decision to end her marriage while in a hospital bed. Friends of the family blamed her heart trouble on her abusive marriage. Bill was a very abusive person. He hit his children, his wife and there was a lot of verbal abuse.

Conclusion:

Child sexual abuse happens to many of our young people. However, it is surrounded by a thick veil of secrecy. Families would rather hush the matter than face the stark truth – that a child in their home is being abused. Victims thus feel as if they are at fault, both for the abuse and the sickness of the family member who abused them. So they suffer in silence.

Chapter 10
HOW TO PREVENT AND STOP CHILD ABUSE

Reporting child abuse

Reporting suspected child abuse is a moral responsibility for everyone in the community. It is also a legal responsibility that any person who has reasonable grounds to believe a child is in need of protective services must report those suspicions. No action may be taken against persons for reporting their suspicions unless the reporting is done maliciously (that is, to purposely hurt another person) or without reasonable and probable grounds for believing that abuse has occurred.

What happens after a report of child sexual abuse?

When a report of suspected abuse is received, a social worker investigates. This should be done immediately if the child's safety is threatened and within three days if the case is not urgent. The purpose of the investigation is to determine whether the child is in need of protective services and if so, what services would be best for the child and his/her family. If at all possible the social worker will work with the child's family and try to improve the situation. Only if the children are in danger will they be removed from their homes immediately and taken to a safe place.

If the situation involves sexual or physical abuse, the police should be informed. All Australian citizens should see this as one of their responsibilities. They should not turn away if they have observed abuse - but should get involved and report the abuse to the police. Only then can the police do their part in stopping the abuse. It is the responsibility of the police to investigate the matter and decide whether criminal charges should be laid. Their concern is to gather evidence and relate it to a possible offender. The social worker's concern is with the well-being of the child. Wherever possible, joint interviews by the police and social worker are arranged.

Many options are available to help the child and, if appropriate, the child's family. The child and/or the family could be referred to a community agency for assistance. Counselling or other support services might be recommended. Removing the child temporarily might be the best thing to do. For more serious cases, the child may need to be given help in a treatment facility.

In some cases, permanent removal from the home may be the best option. In any case involving removal of the child from the home, either temporarily or permanently, the social worker must develop a plan for the child and, if appropriate, the family. If the removal is temporary, the plan must include helping not only the child, but also helping the family to overcome the difficulties they are having in caring for their child. If the removal is permanent, a plan for adoption or some other permanent arrangement must be developed.

Foster parenting

Darlene is a caring foster-parent who took on the care of a newborn who was the child of crack addicted parents. She nurtured the child and got her on track, so that by the time she was three, she was almost normal in her behaviour. She still had fits of rage and unxpected anger episodes, but on the whole she was doing well. Then "the system" sent the child back to her parents (both had been through rehabilitation and supposedly were drug-free).

When the child was four she was again removed from the parents and placed with Darlene. The child was unruly, unmanageable and violent. She would throw things, headbang, swear like a trouper and was completely out-of-control. Darlene struggled with the child for over a year, but because the child was allowed visits with her parents she found it a losing battle. Every time the child was returned to her, the battles began. Finally Darlene had to admit defeat. She knew if she could not control the child at the age of five – how could she control her when she was a teenager? So reluctantly, and with lots of guilt feelings, she had to put the child back into the system.

How to help an abused child

I was doing some grocery shopping when I observed an altercation between a young pre-school-aged boy and his mother. He ran towards her with a can of his favourite soup, but fell heavily near me. He sat up cradling his arm and crying. His mother said, *"Stop being such a sissy - your dad would be so ashamed of you if he heard you."* His mother looked at me and shaking her head said, *"He's such a sissy."*

I patted the child's head and replied, *"I don't think he's a sissy at all. He's just a normal boy who wants and expects love and protection from* you. Instead you've given him more hurt by belittling him in public. Was that what you intended to do?"

"His father is so ashamed of him, I'm trying to toughen him up."

"Do you realise that this is a form of abuse - a misuse of your power position? Children mimic what they observe and will likely pass that bullying attitude on to others because he thinks it's okay to do so."

"I hadn't thought of it that way, but I don't know how to deal with his cowardness."

"Once he feels secure about your love and protection, he won't feel so alone. As it is, he's fighting the entire world on his own - what a lonely place to be."

"How do you know so much about my child's behaviour?"

I told her about all the books I had written and explained about my research for this book. We stopped to have a cup of coffee and before long, her son was cuddling on my lap. He seemed to know instinctively that I would protect him. His mother was surprised to see this, because he was known to "make strange" with other adults.

"He knows he's safe with me." He nodded his head as he gave me another cuddle.

"I can see we've been approaching this problem the wrong way."

"It's important that you understand that this is your problem - not his. He's just wanting and expecting love, protection and nurturing from both his parents."

We discussed what she should say to her husband to change his approach to their son. I asked her whether her husband had a loving nurturing family and learned that the opposite was the case. His father was a real ogre.

"He likely doesn't know that his father was a bully and if he isn't careful, he would be viewed as one himself. Encourage him to use empathy and to remember how he felt when his father bullied him."

"He still responds the same way whenever we're around his father. He hates being with him."

"Ask him if that is what he wants to happen, when his son grows up."

"I'm sure he doesn't and probably isn't aware of what he's doing to our son."

We became friends and it was a pleasure to note the changed interaction between the man and his son. Later the man thanked me for letting him see what he was doing to the fragile ego of his son.

Living with the cost of abuse - Robert Glade-Wright

Robert Glade-Wright is the family law specialist and columnist with the Gold Coast Bulletin. He's a former barrister and now head of family law at Small Myers Hughes. One of his columns entitled; Living with the Cost of Abuse states:

"At the heart of the Family Law Act there's a rather lost direction to the Family Court to 'preserve and protect the institution of marriage,' where really we know the court's role has only ever been to pick up the pieces when a relationship is over. We are soon to be given family relationship centres - being introduced due to the failures of the Family Court. These should offer people a more conducive environment than a courthouse for conciliation. The court will still deal with unresolved disputes and cases of violence, but there is no sign of any change to family law to provide for compensation to be paid by the abuser to the victims of their abuse."

[Author's Note] Why family relationship centres aren't more proactive rather than reactive is beyond me. For years I have suggested that couples be required to attend pre-marital counselling **before** they marry. My own pre-marital workbook; Before Tying the Knot - Questions couples <u>must</u> ask each other <u>before</u> they marry! has proven to be so effective that one out of two couples that complete it honestly find that they're not compatible and decide ***not*** to get married. It has saved many a divorce!

Project Circuit Breaker

A short-term, mobile and free crisis counselling service in Brisbane is operating to try and reduce the number of children and young people experiencing first-time involvement with the Child Protection System or be at imminent risk of furthering their involvement. The service is Mission Australia's Project Circuit Breaker, that receives referrals from the Queensland Department of Child Safety, other government agencies, schools, non-government organisations and the wider community. It aims to:

- Enhance family functioning;
- Improve family resilience;
- Reduce involvement and/or the need for statutory intervention by the Department of Child Safety

Project Circuit Breaker is an early intervention and prevention service for families with children aged 10 to 16 years living in the northern suburbs of Brisbane. Since opening in 2002, it has supported over 800 young people and close to 650 families.

Services Manager, Ray O'Donnell said, *"Family conflict, mental illness, chroming, domestic violence, girls self-harming, boy's anger and severe behavioural problems in children and young people were the main issues the families were confronting."* Youth and Family Development Workers go into the family home or a nominated safe place, rather than having to bring the family into a clinical environment. Learn more about their project at www.missionaustralia.com.au.

Neglect hurts more when you do nothing about it a brochure prepared by Barnardos says: A child is reported abused or neglected every 2 ½ minutes in Australia (The Australian Institute of Health & Welfare). Barnardos Australia believe that neglect is one of the most serious community issues affecting the lives of Australian children. Tragically, over 40% of child deaths and over 50% of physical and sexual assault cases are because of child abuse involving neglect. One of the most likely reasons for a child to be removed from their home by the children's court involves neglect.

Neglect is silent but its effects are violent and long lasting. For over 120 years Barnardos Australia has been listening to traumatised children. By involving these children and young people in planning for their future and finding solutions for them we build new futures. In 2004, Barnardos brought change to the lives of 8,000 children.

Children who are removed from neglectful family situations deserve a chance. For some children there is no hope of helping their families to rear them, their families are too unsafe for these children to survive and grow. Often they have been through many temporary foster homes while the courts finally decide to remove them from their family permanently

For children, these constant changes compound their problems. Unloved and not emotionally nurtured, they need a continuous stable family life. Barnardos Australia's' priority is to find a "forever family" for them.

Barnardos Australia is a non-government and non-denominational agency in Australia that depends on the generosity of the public to continue its vital work. To learn more go to www.barnardos.org.au or call their 24 hour information hotline: 1 800 061 000.

Queensland Government

In June, 2005, Premier Peter Beattie announced that he will provide abused and neglected children with safe homes in a $88 million plan over four years for the carers of vulnerable children. Community agencies said money was desperately needed for early intervention and prevention services to halt the huge number of children coming into state care. At a meeting of 20 representative organisations, they described the child-protection system was in worse shape than before the 2003 Crime and Misconduct Commission inquiry into foster care. After that inquiry the Government gave $250 million (over 3 years) to be spent on setting up a new Child Safety Department. Mr. Beattie said that Queensland has about 3,000 foster carers, we need more. The budget will also provide a multimillion dollar effort to curb chroming or paint sniffing by Queensland youth.

Parents Banned from Smacking Children – February 2005 – *Expatica*

[The rest of the world needs to listen to this new law being implemented in the Netherlands!]

In a proposal that will ban the giving of disciplinary smacks, the Dutch Cabinet has decided to outlaw all forms of violence against children to combat child abuse. Cabinet ministers decided on Friday that parents will in future be explicitly obligated by law to care for their children and to raise them without emotional or physical violence.

An estimated 50,000 to 80,000 children are victims of child abuse each year and several dozen children die as a result of abuse in the home. An investigation into the extent of abuse in the Netherlands will be completed by the end of 2006. Violence and child abuse is already illegal in the Netherlands, but the new law is designed to create a higher sense of values among parents, newspaper NRC reported.

"It's good that everyone will ask themselves: 'Is this violence' It gives an example and a signal to people who can't maintain a standard." Justice Minister Piet Hein said. The minister also said violence does not belong with parenting and asserted further he was not interested in "endless" discussions over parental smacks. "In principle, you should not hand out a smack. A smack often leads to violence." Donner said.

The rulings regarding parental discipline in child abuse cases. The change in legislation will now shift the weight of evidence so that parents cannot simply claim bruises on their children are the result of disciplinary smacks, news agency ANP reported.

Breaches of regulations can lead to supervision from welfare authorities or the loss of custody. In more serious cases, culprits can be jailed at the order of a court.

In several other European countries such as Sweden, Denmark, Germany and Austria – where all forms of violence against children is a criminal offence – evidence is starting to be gathered indicating that the law leads to a reduction in the number of child abuse cases.

How to deal with child bullies

Sometimes child abuse happens with other children – children who are bullies. How do you protect them against child bullying?

"My son throws toys, has tantrums and is generally a tyrant. My friends have stopped bringing their children over, because he's so violent with them. I'm afraid he's turning into a bully."

Most children have temper tantrums to gain attention or to express frustration. This is why the "terrible twos" is often the time when children start resorting to tantrums. Parents must let the child know that such behaviour is unacceptable. The child should be sent to isolation (the opposite of what they had hoped to get by their tirade) and told they can come out when they are ready to behave properly. Do not send the child to his or her bedroom for isolation for two reasons:

1. They will associate the bedroom with punishment and will balk at going to bed at bedtime.
2. There are likely toys there that they can play with. (Isolation places should not have toys near them.)

After they have calmed down, discuss their behaviour and find out what was behind their explosion.

If parents observe their child displaying hurt or angry feelings by willful destruction or excessive anger towards others, the child is possibly a bully or has been bullied. Children display this tendency by throwing things, breaking another's toys, hitting or biting others. It's important to analyse what's behind the child's destructive behaviour. When a child takes delight in torturing animals or other children or if bullying shows up in early life, it's a sure sign that professional help is needed. If children's behaviour is not dealt with before they enter the school system, their destructive pattern may escalate until others (teachers) insist that they obtain professional help.

When children's destruction of an item is deliberate, you can help them handle the results by stressing the rights of others. To start, the child should apologise to the person s/he hurt or whose property was destroyed. Then, identify the costs of repairing the broken item. Children should replace or fix whatever they break. Give a value to tasks they can perform around the house or yard, so they can pay for the damages they've caused. (This is one strong argument in favour of regular allowances for work performed).

If a neighbour's child bullies your child - speak to the bully's parents. Unfortunately, children who are bullies often come from dysfunctional homes and their parents may not cooperate. If serious enough, consider getting the police involved by lodging assault charges on the bully. Often having a police officer reprimand the bully will result in positive changes to the bully's behaviour.

What are the results to the bully?

Primary aged children who are labelled by their peers as bullies:

- Require more support as adults from government agencies;
- Have more court convictions;
- More alcoholism;

- More antisocial personality disorders; and
- Use more mental health services.

Differences between child and adult bullies

There are two main differences:

1. Adult bullies select their targets because they are popular with people (their bullies are weak, inadequate individuals who are driven by jealousy and envy). If there is a child in the class who is socially less popular than the rest, then this child is likely to be targeted by the bully. If no such obvious child exists, then the bully will pick on any child they think is unable or unwilling to fight. A key factor in the bully's choice is any child who is unwilling to resort to violence to resolve conflict - in other words, a child who has integrity and good moral codes. Given that bullies are driven by jealousy and envy - any child who is bright and popular is also likely to be targeted.

   Once bullying starts, many children will side with or appear to side with the bully, because they know that otherwise they themselves will be bullied. The bully is a deeply unpopular child with whom other children associate, not through friendship, but through fear. Many studies, that show bullies are popular, fail to make this distinction. The education system is biased towards physical strength (i.e.: undue emphasis on sport and rewards for sporting achievement) while artistic achievements are undervalued.

   Children (and adults) who are bullied tend to be imaginative, creative, caring and responsible. Children (and adults) who bully are unimaginative, uncaring, aggressive, emotionally immature, inadequate (especially in social skills) and irresponsible.

   There is a lot anecdotal evidence to suggest that the child who learns to bully at school and gets away with it, goes on to be the serial bully in the workplace. The evidence suggests that the child who is bullied at school also goes on to be a likely target of bullying in the workplace. This has nothing to do with being predisposed to being bullied - it has to do with the innate qualities of good people.

2. By the time a person enters adulthood at around the age of 18, his/her behaviour pattern is set and only time or a traumatic

experience can alter these patterns. However, people who are likely to be bullied have a considerable learning capability and thus have a greater capacity than bullies to modify their behaviour as an adult. People who are bullies or prone to have limited learning capacity (especially in interpersonal and behavioural skills) will often exhibit bullying behaviours for the rest of their lives. Emotionally, the bully remains a young child and his/her attention-seeking behaviour is characteristic of a two-year-old throwing a temper tantrum in order to gain attention. Serial bullies have psychopathic or sociopathic tendencies that include a learning blindness and an apparent lack of insight into their behaviour and its effect on others. The second major difference between adult and child bullying is that the child bully can be helped to develop better ways of behaving. This is where society needs to place its emphasis - on helping these children develop into better adults.

Dealing with Child Bullies

Adults in the bullying child's life need to:

- Concentrate on giving rewards for good behaviour rather than punishing for bad behaviour;
- Educate the child on how to show respect for others and their possessions;
- Show them the difference between passive, assertive and aggressive behaviour;
- Regularly assure them of your love.

Dealing with the victim:

"My eight-year-old son is anxious and unhappy. He complains of tummy aches with no medical cause, resists going to school and his grades are dropping. He's having nightmares and cries at the slightest incident. He finally explained that a boy at school was pushing and shoving him and trying to make him fight. How can I help him deal with bullies?"

Bullies get a kick out of upsetting others and beating them up. Their victims are often quiet, suffer in silence and don't seek help. Bullies are visible, so they usually get counselling, but their victims are the unseen problem.

Start by having a discussion with your son's teachers. If the teacher is un-cooperative, speak to the principal. Both the victim and the bully should be counselled.

Some elementary schools help these bullied children by offering special clinics for them. They act out "bully" parts where they're subjected to name-calling and teasing, so they can learn effective measures when dealing with aggressive playmates. Often the role-playing situations are from problems experienced by one of the group members.

The classes concentrate on building the self-esteem level of children, which helps them send the message that *"I'm not someone you can easily victimise."* It becomes easier for them to tell other students to stop teasing them or walk away from threatening situations without feeling like a failure.

One Canadian city is having police officers speak at schools explaining the consequences of bullying. They also address the students about the unacceptability of standing by when they observe bullying - that they must stop it or at least report it. No longer is it acceptable to either bully others or stand by and watch it happening.

Students who get into fights at school sign a contract with the police officer, the school and the parents involved that they will straighten out, otherwise they'll be charged by the police. Others sign contracts that they will do their homework, behave at home and write a paper about being assertive without being violent.

One last resort for parents is to contemplate getting the police involved by lodging assault charges against the bully. Often having a police officer reprimand the bully results in positive changes in the bully's behaviour. Do everything you can, before resorting to changing schools for your child.

"My seven-year-old son has changed behaviour drastically in the past month. He's gone from being a well-adjusted happy boy; to one who's behaviour swings between throwing tantrums and withdrawal. How can we investigate this without making matters worse?"

Talk about the behaviour he's displaying and ask him (in a non-threatening way) what's happening. *"It's not like you to have tantrums and get angry this way. What's happening to make you so angry?"*

Do the same for his symptoms of withdrawal. You might find that he's facing serious problems either at school or with his peer group. These behaviours can often be a sign that someone at school is bullying the child. The suppressed anxiety and anger at his predicament could be demonstrated as tantrums at home. This is likely an environment where he feels safer in expressing his anxiety, frustration and anger. Knowing you care about him, will start you both on the way to solving his problem.

If he clams up, talk to his teacher and even his friends about his behaviour so you'll know what hidden problems exist for your son. Don't let the situation slide or his behaviour is likely to worsen. Consider getting professional counselling if the above attempts do not correct the behaviour.

Note: To learn more about school bullying - watch for my book entitled: *"Dealing with School Bullying Society's Educational Disgrace!"*

Conclusion:

Although society has a role to play in controlling child abuse, the ultimate responsibility rests with the parents. They are urged to not sit by while their child either bullies or shows signs that they have been bullied. They need to deal with the situation by either confronting the unacceptable behaviour or by providing the needed support. In some cases the child may need professional help and parents should not be afraid to take this step.

Chapter 11
GOOD PARENTING

Super Nanny! www.b4ugo-ga-ga.co.uk

The television program Super Nanny has made a big impact on its viewers and Jo Frost's book ***Supernanny - How to get the best from your children*** is destined to be a best-seller world-wide. Her program had an audience of 1.86 million viewers when it first came to Australia and her impact is immense. Jo goes into family homes and does three things:

1. She observes;
2. She advises;
3. She transforms.

Her tools for dealing with unacceptable behaviour work both on the screen and off and involve another three things:

a. Routine;
b. Respect;
c. Consequences for misbehaviour.

Jo introduced the "Naughty Spot Technique" (that could be a naughty step, mat or stool) where the child goes when s/he is using unacceptable behaviour. She prevents fussy eaters from taking over at mealtime, stops the "supermarket game," resolves children's sleep problems, avoids sibling rivalry battles, establishes a routine that works for the family and bridges the gap between parents and children. So they will listen, she encourages parents to go down to the child's level when speaking with them - especially when disciplining.

Her program isn't about controlling kids, but about training parents who have abandoned or don't understand their responsibilities. She puts honour back into the role of parenting. Mom and Dad are shown that their roles are as educators and authority figures that must be obeyed. She encourages parents to work as a team. It causes parents to look at the long-term benefits of enforcing discipline for unacceptable behaviour.

Jo states that happy families are the result of hard work. Children without guidance will simply do what they want and will rule the roost if given too many choices.

The only criticism I have of her methods is that she labels children rather than discussing the behaviour of the children. Children are not naughty - their behaviour is.

Battling Children

When should parents step in to break up arguments between two children? Try to get your children to solve their own differences unless they've become physically or emotionally aggressive towards one another. If that happens, separate them and take steps to stop the behaviour from happening in the future. Look behind the behaviour to see why they're acting the way they are. Do they feel left out? Aggressive behaviour is often the way children express damaged feelings, because they don't know any other way to express their frustration.

Tantrums

"My daughter is four and still has temper tantrums. Some little disappointment happens and she's stamping her foot and screaming."

When children lose their tempers and express their anger in inappropriate ways, it's important to look beyond the outburst to detect what caused it. You'll notice that behind every outburst is some negative feeling the child is trying to cope with. You can help your children learn how to cope with their negative feelings.

For instance, if you told your daughter to go to bed and she resorted to a tantrum, you might find that she was in the middle of an important game with her older brother (she was winning). This doesn't mean you give in to the tantrum. Instead explain that if she had told you about the importance of the game, instead of screaming at you, you might have allowed her to finish the game.

Point out that everyone has to deal with occasional embarrassing or frustrating situations. Because she had a tantrum (instead of explaining her need to finish the game) she'll have to go to bed without a bedtime story (or another withdrawal of privileges).

Never reward unacceptable behaviour with privileges.

If she has tantrums in public, remove her immediately. Explain that in the future, she will have to stay with a babysitter and miss special excursions because of her behaviour. This tactic is especially effective if there are other well-behaved children who will accompany the parents while the errant child stays home with a babysitter. This way, the errant child will receive isolation - the opposite of what s/he was hoping to obtain by having a tantrum.

The Terrible Two's

"My two-year-old is very bright, but still can't put sentences together. She's prone to having tantrums, especially when she doesn't get her way."

She's going through the "terrible two's." This is a very frustrating time for toddlers. They try and try to communicate with us, but we don't understand what they're trying to tell us. I compare this inability to communicate to an adult who has had a stroke that affects his/her speech. How frustrating this must be for both these individuals!

Parents need to give more time and effort into trying to understand what their toddlers are trying to communicate. This extra effort will reap many benefits - a happier toddler and an end to the tantrums caused by the toddler's communication frustrations.

One new method that's proving to be very effective is to teach babies sign language or giving them physical ways of asking for what they want. (i.e.: Have them pretend to be drinking a glass of water, when they're thirsty).

Street-proofing your child

"My biggest fear is that my child will go out to play and simply disappear. How can I keep myself from panicking whenever my child is out of my sight?"

You've just described a parent's worst nightmare. Headlines often shock parents into taking emergency measures. Parents forbid their children to visit parks on their own, walk them to and from school and warn them repeatedly about not talking or going with strangers. Unfortunately, overreacting parents can alarm children needlessly. So what's the answer? It's street-proofing your children. They won't learn this by running at the sight of a stranger. They require tools to enable them to determine for themselves when a situation isn't right.

When your children are old enough to play with friends on their own, ensure they understand that you must always know where they are.

Having your children call you when they're leaving their playmates' homes will enable you to watch for them as they travel home. You might ask the other mothers to call you before your children leave or else walk them home.

When your children understand what to call body parts, make sure they know their body is theirs alone and they have permission to refuse any touching that feels uncomfortable. They're to tell you immediately if this happens. Street-proofing your children includes:

- Asking them such questions as, *"What would you do if a stranger offered to give you a puppy or ice cream cone if you would go with them?"* Define clearly what a stranger is. For instance, the mailman they see every day is not necessarily someone they know.
- Teaching them the different lures (puppy, ice cream cone) and not to accept gifts from people they don't know.
- Encouraging them to be with a buddy.
- Establishing a code word to be used in emergencies.
- Making sure they know their address and telephone number and to never say they're alone if they answer the phone.
- Telling them they should not invite anyone into their home without the permission of a parent or babysitter.
- Encouraging them not to go into people's houses or vehicles without letting someone know and to move away from a car that pulls up beside them if they don't know the driver.
- Cautioning them not to play in deserted buildings or isolated areas.
- Advising them to scream and scatter books and belongings if they're forced towards a building or car.
- Promising to tell you if someone has asked them to keep a secret from you.
- Warning older children never to hitchhike or take shortcuts through fields or alleys.
- If they're attacked for money, jeweler or clothing - to give them up, rather than risk injury.
- Calling you anytime to pick them up if they're in trouble (without a hassle).
- Making sure your children know whom they could go to for help - police officers, block parents and teachers. Contact Block Parent or Child Find organisations for specifics.

- Discussing what they should do, if they become lost in a store or wander away from home.

Street-Smart Kids

There are many good books and videos available to help parents and children develop street smarts and safety skills. Most are free in libraries and many video stores.

Videos include:

- Kids Safe (when to call 911 (000), first aid, fire & safety, handling strangers).
- Strong Kids, Safe Kids (strangers, child abuse and abductions).
- Kids have Rights Too (child abuse, privacy, carefree childhood).

Books include:

- Benjamin Rabbit and the Stranger Danger, by Irene Keller.
- Play it Safe, by Kathy Kyte.
- Who is This Stranger and What Should I do? By Linda Girard.
- How to Raise a Street-Smart Child, by Grace Hechinger.

How can you help?

- Establish parent education, support, relief and treatment services in your communities;
- Promote child development, human relations and positive parenting courses in schools;
- Encourage public education about child abuse in your community;
- Ensure that professionals receive training so they can recognise and respond to abuse problems appropriately;
- Support women and child shelters;
- Work diligently to see that the laws are changed to protect the abused - laws that remove the abuser (not the family) from the family home.

What to do if you need to leave your children at home alone:

Occasionally parents must leave their children at home and especially during the summer holidays when they must work. The child in charge should be at least thirteen years of age (a mature thirteen) otherwise a child carer should be hired. Here are some basic rules:

- Talk to them first about any fears they may have about being alone. Tell them where you will be. Explain and write down what to do in case of an emergency.
- Check that safety equipment such as fire extinguishers and door locks are working.
- Reassure them that it's okay to call you at work. Let your employer know your children may be calling you at work.
- List important phone numbers next to the phone or on the fridge. Call your children during the day to see how they are. Teach your children how to take phone messages without letting callers know they are home alone.
- Let neighbours know your children are home alone. Ask a friend or relative to check on them during the day.
- Put together a first-aid kit.
- Set rules, such as when they are allowed to go out and whether they can have friends over.
- Think of strategies to keep them occupied and relieve boredom.
- Safety-proof your home by locking medications and household chemicals away from toddlers.

Out of Control Teens

Domestic violence is not always between husbands and wives. Some teens become abusive to their parents, siblings or friends. What's a parent to do?

Many community and counselling programs help troubled teens. If you find your teen is not responding to your efforts to help, call in professional re-enforcement. One community program that's been successful, pairs a model student with a teen in trouble. Trained counsellors monitor the teens' progress. The volunteer model student provides anything from help with homework, to companionship and a shoulder to cry on.

Today it often seems that the children have all the rights. Tough Love groups advocate that parents have rights too. This organisation has helped many parents who have incorrigible teens. It is a support group for parents. These groups are not there to blame anyone, because at this point, it doesn't matter what caused the problem. The issue is - how to solve the situation.

Find your nearest Tough Love group and attend a meeting. Parents can examine the following criteria to find out if they need the help of Tough Love. The key to the Tough Love approach is letting children be responsible for their own behaviour and the consequences of that behaviour. Parents need to set a "Bottom Line" - something they want to accomplish with their teenager. It might be something as simple as insisting they take out the garbage.

Assess your situation by checking any items in the following lists that describe your situation:

Your teenager has run away:
- Overnight;
- For two days;
- For a week;
- For more than a week.

Your teenager has:
- Missed dinner;
- Been late;
- Been stoned or drunk;
- Didn't come home at all;
- Overnight;
- For two days
- For a week;
- For more than a week;

At Home:
- You and your spouse argue about your teenager's behaviour.
- You have withdrawn from your spouse.
- Your spouse has withdrawn from you.
- You have not had a peaceful night's sleep.
- You hate to hear the phone ring when your teenager is not home.
- You or your spouse have lost time from work because of your teenager.

At school, your teenager has been:
- Tardy;
- Absent;
- Playing hooky;

- Suspended;
- You've been called by the school for bad behaviour;

Your teenager has been violent:
- Verbally;
- Physically to the house or furniture;
- Physically to you, your spouse or your children
- Physically to other people;
- In school;
- With the police;

Legally, your teenager has:
- Received summons;
- Received fines;
- Received tickets;
- Been involved in accidents;
- Been charged with drug incidents;
- Been charged with drinking;
- Been arrested;

If you've checked two areas in the school category, two areas in the home category and one area in the legal category, the crisis is building. If you've checked more areas, you're already in crisis and should contact your local Tough Love group for help. They can help when parents have tried everything else from police to social services and find traditional methods don't work. Do it now, your family's future depends on it.

Disciplining when angry

Many parents wonder if they too may slip over the edge and become child abusers. These are parents who may have children who are truly difficult to handle. The child's negative behaviour includes aggressiveness, is whiny, picky, defiant, stubborn, loud and disruptive in public. Some children are born that way and it's not their parent's fault. The child isn't working at being a difficult child. They're born with these traits that make them hard to raise. One or both parents were usually hard to raise themselves. Many of these children show the following characteristics. They:

- Are hyperactive, can't sit still for more than a few minutes at a time;

- Have short attention spans;
- Are easily distracted;
- Appear over-stimulated or oversensitive to their environment but are insensitive to the feelings of others;
- Withdraw from others;
- Are extremely moody;
- Seldom understand the consequences of their negative behaviour;
- Show stubbornness and persistence that things must go their own way;
- Cheat at games;
- Get into trouble at school and later with the law;
- Are perfectionists;
- Are easily frustrated;
- Show great disappointment even with small setbacks;
- Have problems adjusting to change of any kind.

These children can drive adults to distraction. To cope effectively, parents must first like their children. This differs from loving them. Liking their children, stems from acceptance of them as they are, with all their warts and behavioural patterns. This needs patience, understanding and empathy in parents. Without this empathy the battle is likely to continue.

Many parents admit they're on different wave lengths than that of their children. They don't understand why they do what they do and resort to control methods and punishment to get the errant child to behave. This seldom works and often triggers further negative behaviour from the child.

Some of these children are experts at pitting parents against each other. The parents' different disciplinary styles can in turn affect the child's sense of balance. Poor parental direction, combined with the difficult behaviour, leads to a vicious circle. Negative behaviour meets with negative reaction and the participants become locked into a consistent negative situation. Parents and children both feel as if they're victims. The tension the child initiates can cause the marriage to flounder.

Unfortunately, parents make comments in the heat of the moment, little realising that their negative comments can be "locked-in" for part or all their child's life. So how are parents to deal with this kind of situation?

Try to understand why your child acts the way s/he does. Communicate. Have dialogue with your child. Don't make the interview an inquisition where you back him/her into a corner making him/her explain why s/he does what s/he does. Often the child doesn't know why either.

Don't speak on impulse. Walk away for a minute or take yourself away mentally for a moment and think of something other than the problem. Count to ten.

Use humour whenever possible to control your anger. For example picture yourself tossing an imaginary cream pie in your child's face if s/he does something to make you angry. This will defuse your anger and keep your objectivity.

Set guidelines the child can meet. Discuss these guidelines with the child and get his or her input about where s/he would like some leeway.

Read everything you can about manipulation and the games people play to get their way.

Learn coping tactics to overcome negative reactions to game playing.

Try to remain objective. Deal with the child rationally, rather than emotionally. Walk away from the situation if necessary until you've calmed down. Putting the child in isolation in the meantime might be best for you both. Make sure the child understands that you aren't abandoning them, but will discuss the problem later when you've both calmed down. In the meantime, write down what the child has done, how you felt about it and what you're willing to do about it.

The child has misbehaved, so the parent says, *"I don't want to talk to you any more."* Most children hate isolation. Little do parents realise that the pre-school child feels frightened by this perceived abandonment by their parent. Their silent treatment is very cruel punishment. Instead, the parent would be wise to send the child to another room with the comment, *"When you're ready to behave properly, you can come back."* This gives the control of the isolation to the child without the terrifying sense of abandonment. Make sure the punishment is worse than the original situation. For instance, don't send the child to a room full of toys otherwise s/he'll be playing during punishment.

Concentrate on your child's positive behaviour. Most children want to please, but if the only way they perceive they can get your attention is to be bad, that's what you'll get from them. Try talking calmly about the situation. If that doesn't work, (rather than yelling or hitting them) give them isolation for their bad behaviour or start removing privileges.

Don't over-react, by saying or doing something you'll regret. For instance, think of a time when a child tripped, fell down and broke something. Yelling at him or her for breaking the item is double punishment if the child hurt him or herself when s/he fell.

Develop responses to familiar problems and strive to use them. If the child balks, you'll have to determine the consequences to the child's actions. Make sure you follow-through with the action. For instance, if Johnnie hits his brother, tell him that he can't watch his favourite television program if he does it again in the future. Try to teach him how to deal with the situation that led to the hitting of his brother. Communicate, listen and be willing to hear his side of the situation.

If you find you can't change the negative behaviour, by all means discuss the problems with a child psychologist or get family counselling so the whole family can deal with the child's difficult behaviour.

To spank or not to spank?

Spanking is a swat on the child's bottom; hitting anywhere else is considered abusive. Have you ever spanked your child? For five decades, child-rearing professionals have preached against spanking for discipline. Not only does it hurt, but it also starts negative psychological effects and can be a forerunner to child abuse. One or two spankings in childhood are not going to be damaging, but it's hard to know the limit between discipline and abuse.

The purpose of discipline is not simply to punish, but to teach. Spanking only punishes and seldom teaches. Spanking stops unwanted action but works only because of the child's fear and loss of trust in the spanker. A child who gets a spanking (no matter how light) can become too upset to hear what parents say. Physical punishment undermines anything else the parent might do, however positive.

If children see their parents are out of control, they seldom learn self-control themselves and lash out at others physically. Children who receive frequent spankings are more aggressive throughout their lives. They often become child bullies and adult criminals.

The worst kind of spanking involves the use of some type of tool, be it a wooden spoon, belt or hairbrush. Children can't help believe that people who are bigger than they, can get away with physical aggression. When parents are angry, think of what that angry, contorted face must look like to a two-year-old. It would stop most adults in their tracks.

Then how do you deal with bratty, defiant and downright frustrating children? There are alternatives to spanking. Any form of discipline that breaks the cycle of unacceptable behaviour is preferable to spanking. One is the use of warnings, but make sure you follow-through with what you say you're going to do if they misbehave again.

For many children, a stern tone or a raised eyebrow is sufficient after they've learned to trust their parents and know that punishment for bad behaviour will be fair.

Skill of feedback

Use feedback for both positive and negative reactions. Give positive feedback through recognition and compliments by letting your children know when you like something they've said or done. These comments make them feel good about themselves. Unfortunately, most of us ignore the good things children do or say and concentrate on only the bad. Because this section is about dealing with difficult children's behaviour, we'll be concentrating only on using it under negative or difficult situations, but don't forget the importance of positive feedback.

In feedback, you share your reactions to another person's behaviour, with that person. Use negative feedback if something your child has done has upset or irritated you. Discuss how you feel when they act or behave a certain way. Children can't try to change their behaviour unless you let them know what their actions are doing to you.

You're not being fair to others if you don't communicate this to them. Letting negative situations build up, only escalates the difficulties between you. Resolve minor difficulties when they occur, don't just collect them for future blowups.

If we don't practice effective feedback, the following often results:

Every time the child does anything that bothers you, a small blip occurs on your "screen of annoyance." If you don't deal with the problem or situation and the child repeats his/her behaviour, this leads to;

Another, bigger blip occurring on your "screen of annoyance." This does NOT have to be for the same reason as the original irritation.

Soon these blips collect and you have a major blow-up with the child.

Even the most trivial incident can trigger this response. How much better it would be if we handled each irritant immediately, instead of recording it on our "screen of annoyance." Feedback should be used when we:

- Feel they have misbehaved;
- Don't understand something they've said or done;
- Disagree with them;
- Are getting irritated;
- Feel out of control.

By using feedback, we can keep in touch with our feelings and can lessen problems associated with more serious negative feelings such as, frustration and anger.

When I observe some families, I wonder who is in charge. The child whines, cries, has temper tantrums and the parents give in to the pint-sized tyrant. It's sad to see three-year-olds ruling a home. Their parents are heard to say, *"For the fourteenth time, will you stop doing that!"*

These parents haven't learned the feedback technique that advocates - three strikes you're out. This process should be started when the child is two so s/he learns how to accept the consequences for his/her actions. (I know many fifty-year-olds who have never learned this concept.) The only way children learn this is if the parent lets them know what the consequences will be if they continue doing what they're doing. For example: It's bedtime and you want your two-year-old son to pick up his toys. As usual he ignores you. Here are the feedback steps you should take to deal with his behaviour:

a. Describe the problem or situation to the person/child causing the difficulty: *"Johnny, it's bedtime. It's time to pick up your toys."*
b. Define what feelings or reactions their behaviour causes you (sadness, anger, anxiety, hurt or upset). *"Mommy doesn't think she should be the one to pick up your toys."*
c. Suggest a solution or ask them to provide one. *"So let's see how fast you can pick them up."*

If his behaviour doesn't change:

1. Follow (a), (b) and (c) steps from process of feedback. If person/child ignores you:
2. Repeat #1. (Optional).
3. (i) Ask child to explain why s/he's still doing something that s/he knows annoys you. (The child must be old enough to understand this concept).
   (ii) Explain the consequences should the behaviour or situation happens again.
4. Follow-through with the consequences.

Explain the consequences that will occur if he doesn't pick up his toys. *"If you don't pick up your toys, they will go into a plastic bag and you won't be able to play with them for a month."* Make sure you follow through - and no weakening before the month is up.

Everyone who cares for the child must follow this technique, otherwise the child will start playing one person against the other. So be sure to discuss this with all child caregivers.

Children who learn this life skill will not turn out to the rulers of the home and won't require "tough love" sessions to correct bad behaviour when they're teenagers. Start now - don't let a day go by if your children are the rulers of your home.

Punishment for young children needs to be consistent and immediate. Make sure the child knows how s/he stepped over the limits and that the punishment is the consequence. The simple understanding of cause and effect (consequences) is one of the most important concepts children can learn. The sooner children learn this philosophy, the less trouble they will have as they grow up.

After Discipline

Parents may find problems occur after they find it necessary to discipline their child. After the discipline, they may want to make sure their children know they still love them, even if they have misbehaved. They try to express their feelings by hugging their children, but often the children pull away and won't let their parents touch them. This can result in a defensive reaction in the parents.

The parents need to be patient, because later, the children will likely allow hugs. The parents should watch for non-verbal signs of acceptance from their children that shows they're ready for comforting. They may show this by simply re-entering the room where the parents are sitting.

Preparing your child for society

Doting parents can do their child more harm than good. Timid children may simply be attention junkies who need more and more of their parents' time. The phrase "timid" child is usually used to refer to a child who lives without adequate protection, guidance and love. "Timid" has evolved into a catchall we tend to group children under if they're too quiet to be hyperactive and do too well in school to be classed as learning disabled. But they still drive their parents crazy. The parents want to know how they can make their child feel more secure.

For many, the problem is that these are first children and the parents dote on their every whim. The symptoms vary, but are generally those of a passive, overly-dependent child. These children are incessant talkers, who can't tolerate the slightest frustration and most wake up at night with nightmares. Timid children:

- Cry and whine a lot;
- Have difficulty making friends;
- Want to sleep with their parents;
- Believe they're incompetent - or can't do anything right;
- Interrupt every adult conversation with his/her chatter;
- Suck their thumbs;
- Are fearful of everyday things like their closet; or
- Do things that are equally puzzling and unsettling to their parents

The popular assumption is that their timidity is caused by a lack of proper attention and can therefore be cured by giving more of that. Giving a timid child enormous amounts of attention will not help. But what will? More often than not, the child whose behaviour seems to be the most timid, is the very child who needs drastically less attention than s/he's been receiving.

Treatment of these children can be hard on the parents. They should start by telling their child to talk less and send the child to another room to calm down when s/he begins to chatter incessantly or interrupts adult conversation. A timer is set for five minutes and s/he can emerge when the bell goes off. In most cases, nothing more needs to be done. Most children's chatter ceases almost immediately - and so do their nightmares. And the child stops crying about minor frustrations and saying s/he is incompetent.

The supposedly timid child's symptoms of insecurity disappear after parents set reasonable limits on some established, annoying aspect of their child's behaviour. This shows that many so-called "timid" children are lacking - not in love and attention - but in discipline. It also affirms that effective discipline is at least as important as love to a child's sense of security.

What do children need from their parents?

Children need more from their parents than food on the table and clothes in the closet. Feeling loved is an important part of a child's overall health. It's something all human beings require. A father's kiss should fit as comfortably on the cheek of a son as on that of a daughter. Most parents have problems expressing those feelings - especially the fathers. Most men grew up never having heard their father's say, *"I love you."* And most never expressed that feeling to their fathers - even when they were dying.

Many people were raised that way. Men and women were raised by parents who loved them but never said so. However our generation has devoted a great deal of attention to getting in touch with our feelings and to verbalise our emotions.

One father didn't know how to react at first when his thirteen-year-old suddenly stated to him, *"I love you."* But when his son said goodnight that evening, he held on to him for an extra second. Just before his son pulled away he said in his deepest, most manly voice, *"Hey, I love you too."* The father felt very good and vowed that the next time one of his children said, *"I love you,"* it wouldn't take him an entire day to think of what he should reply.

Conclusion:

The safest route we have against child abuse is for parents to first deal with their own issues. Then parents should show their children an appropriate balance of love and affection on one hand and consistent discipline on the other. This will ensure that the children will avoid becoming bullies themselves and be better situated to resist any paedophiles who may seek and prey upon them. Ultimately, it will also lead to the breaking of the cycle of violence that traps so many families.

CONCLUSION

The saying goes, *"A man's home is his castle,"* but many men act as if they are feudal lords and behave accordingly. A home should be a sanctuary, where people can live peacefully and more importantly - safely. Those who break this unwritten code of society should be punished severely. Our efforts should be spent making a home the sanctuary it should be for every member of the family.

The Australian government will be funding more mediation services for couples whose marriages are in jeopardy. That's fine. But why are they not making it mandatory for couples to have pre-marital counselling that will help to determine what each of them think is "normal" family behaviour. This way, those who have been brought up to believe that conflict should be solved with violence and abuse will be identified and hopefully will be made to understand that they require counselling or they will continue the cycle of abuse.

Australian laws relating to domestic violence and child abuse are in desperate need of revision. All Australian women need to know that each state's laws will give them the same protection, so uniformity of those laws is paramount.

The Police are doing all they can, but presently, domestic violence abusers receive little more than a slap on the wrist by the courts. We could learn a lesson from The Netherlands. Their Government intends to create ways of imposing temporary restraining orders for perpetrators of domestic violence and child abuse in situations where there is an acute threat to victims and/or any children. Their Government is working on a ten-day restraining order that will be imposed by the police with the mayor's consent. The court would test the order within three days after its commencement date and decide whether the order should be cancelled, reinforced or extended for a maximum period of four weeks.

Punishments in Australia should be far more severe, so the abusers are discouraged from committing future battering or child abuse. The more the battering - the higher the jail sentence should be. And some should be classified as habitual criminals and locked up for life.

It's interesting to note that if two neighbours were involved in a dispute and one was bashed - the penalty would be quite severe and yet if a husband gives the same injury to his wife or hurts his children, he gets a judicial slap on the wrist and likely continues his abuse.

Right now, if the police are called to deal with a domestic violence situation, they will likely assist the innocent women and children leave their homes - but in many cases, the abusers are allowed to stay. This doesn't make sense! The abusers are the criminals and should be forced to leave the home - not innocent family members. In addition, the abusers should immediately receive restraining orders to stay away from their wives and children. Breach of those orders should be swift and severely punished by the courts.

Another possibility is to have the abuser put in an "abuser's shelter" where he would be incarcerated until his trial. In cases of serious battering, abusers should be given jail sentences relating to the level of abuse. Part of the sentence should be that they are forced to attend counselling sessions and not be released from prison until the counsellor was convinced that they'd changed their attitude towards battering.

Healthcare workers are now required to report suspected child abuse, but are not required to do so in cases of suspected domestic violence. They should also have to report suspected domestic violence cases.

In an ideal world, when police are called to an obvious domestic violence and/or abuse situation they should charge the abuser and not make the battered wife or family member do so. Many battered individuals are too afraid to charge the abuser, because they're afraid of more retaliation. If the police charged the abuser, the battered wife would have one less problem to face when seeking release from her abuser.

Assaulted women are usually required to appear in court to testify. Shelter workers, court workers and victim service units should guide the assaulted woman through the legal system and be there to protect her against more abuse. Many women face this trauma alone.

In cases where a stranger commits child rape or abuse, society deals with it immediately and ruthlessly. But if a father, brother or mother commits the child rape or abuse, s/he rarely faces a jail term. If s/he receives a sentence, it's trivial when compared to stranger-child rape or abuse. This MUST change! If the situation involves sexual or physical abuse, the police should be informed. It is their responsibility to investigate the matter and decide whether criminal charges should be laid.

Women who smoke during their pregnancy and parents who subject their children to second-hand smoke should also be charged formally with child abuse.

We must demand that our politicians and courts toughen up our legal system so that society (and the laws) have zero-tolerance to any violent act. The rest of the world needs to listen to a new law being implemented in the Netherlands where the Dutch Cabinet has decided to outlaw all forms of violence against children to combat child abuse. Parents are explicitly obligated by law to care for their children and to raise them without emotional or physical violence.

Until such zero-tolerance laws are enforced, the peaceful citizens of Australia will not be properly protected from the violent and abusive behaviour that seems to permeate our country. It still amazes me that someone caught with illegal drugs can be jailed for 12 years and if drug smuggling 25 years, yet the wife and child batterers just get a slap on the wrist and are freed to continue their mayhem.

The cycle of abuse must end. Only by keeping the public aware of the travesties being committed against wives and children, will a solution be found. Australia's macho image needs serious revision - the beating of wives and/or children is not masculine - it's cowardice. The police need more power to stop this abuse and the courts must ensure that those responsible for domestic violence and child abuse are given sentences similar to those who hurt others.

I firmly believe that the lack of prevention and proper sentencing for those accused of Domestic Violence and Child Abuse is Society's Judicial Disgrace! Changing our legal system is the only answer!

BIBLIOGRAPHY

David Kinchin: ***Post Traumatic Stress Disorder - The Invisible Injury***, Success Unlimited, U.K.2001.

Neil Marr & Tim Field***: Bullycide Death at Playtime – An expose of child suicide caused by bullying***, Success Unlimited, U.K. 2001.

David Fulton: ***Supporting Children with Post-traumatic Stress Disorder: A practical guide for teachers and professionals***: David Fulton Publishers.

M. Napier & K. Wheat: ***Recovering damages for psychiatric injury:*** Blackstone Press.

Dr. William Wilkie***: Understanding Stress Breakdown:*** Millennium Books, 1995.

V. Sutherland & C. Cooper: ***Understanding Stress:*** Chapman & Hall

Tedeschi & L. Calhoun: ***Trauma & Transformation; growing in the aftermath of suffering:*** Sage, 1996.

Sam Vaknim: ***Malignant Self-Love – Narcissism Revisited***

Hervey Cleckley: ***The Mask of Sanity***: CV Mosby Publishers, 1976.

Stanton E. Samenow***: Straight Talk about Criminals – Inside the Criminal Mind.***

Michele Elliott: ***501 Ways to be a good parent;*** Hodder. and ***Keeping Safe, a practical guide to talking with children***: Coronet Books, 1994; and ***The Willow Street Kids: Be smart, stay safe:*** Pan Macmillan; and ***The Willow Street Kids: Beat the bullies:*** Pan Macmillan; and ***Bullying: a practical guide for coping for schools***: FT Prentice Hall; and ***Female sexual abuse of children: the ultimate taboo***; John Wiley.

Michele Elliott & Gaby Shenton: ***Bully Free: Kidscape***, Bracher Giles & Martin, 1999.

Patricia Evans: ***The verbally abusive relationship; how to recognise it and how to respond***: Adams.

Cindy Seddon & Cindy Lowrey: ***Take Action Against Bullying.***

Sherryl Kraiser, PhD: ***The Safe Child Book.***

Jo Frost: Supernanny – ***How to get the best from your children.***

Robert D. Hare: ***Without Conscience, The disturbing world of psychopaths among us:*** The Gilford Press, 1999; and ***Work Rage:*** (Narcissist Manager) Canada; and ***The Magic of Believing – Getting Up when You're Down***; and ***Kiss Daddy Goodnight:*** Pocket Books; and ***Making Peace with your parents:*** Ballantyne Books, NY.

Wayne Dyer: ***You'll see it when you believe it:*** Bantam Books; and ***Men who hate women – the women who love them***: Bantam Books; and ***Toxic Parents***: Bantam Books; and ***Your Eroneous Zones***; and ***The Sky's The Limit;*** and ***Smart women – foolish choices***: New American Library.

Dale Carnege: ***Free From Fears***: Pocket Book; and ***Snow White Syndrome***: Jove Books, Berkley Pub Group.

Catherine Clout-Habel: ***Work Abuse – How to recognise it;*** and ***Work Abuse – How to recognise and survive it.***

Keith Sullivan: ***The Anti-Bullying Handbook;*** Oxford University Press, 2000.

Barrie Levy: ***Dating Violence: Young Women in Danger.***

Irene Keller: ***Benjamin Rabbit and the Stranger Danger.***

Kathy Dyte: ***Play it Safe.***

Linda Girard: ***Who is this stranger and what should I do?***

Grace Hechinger: ***How to raise a Street-Smart child.***

Lenore Walker: ***The Battered Woman.***

Doreen Orion, MD (Stalking): ***I know you really love me.***

Dorothea M. Ross, PhD: ***Childhood Bullying and Teasing: What school personnel, other professionals and parents can do.***

Desa Acaster: ***Strategies for Developing Empathy in Children.***

Thomas Crum: ***The Magic Conflict***: Simon & Schuster, 1987.

Naomi Drew: ***Learning Skills of Peacemaking:*** Jalmar Press, California, 1987.

Kath & Roc, Margaret Hawke: ***Conflict Resolution:*** Macmillan Education, Australia, 1992.

Jane Nelsen: ***Positive Discipline***, Ballantine Books, 1987.

Alan Pease: ***Body Language – How to Read Others' Thoughts by their gestures***: Carmel Publications, 1981.

D. Olweus: ***Bullying at School: What we know and what we can do***, Oxford Blackwell Publishers, 1993.

S. Sharp & P. Smith: ***Tackling Bullying in Your School***, Routledge, London, 1994.

Steel, Danielle; ***Journey:*** Bantam Press, 2000.

Rosemary Stones: ***Don't Pick on Me***, Piccadilly Press, 1993.

Revor Romain; ***Bullies are a pain in the brain;*** Free Spirit Publishing, 1997.

Barbara Coloroso: ***The Bully, The Bullied and the Bystander***; Harper Collins.

Evelyn Field: ***Bully Busting***; Finch, 1999.

Vivette O'Donnell: ***Bullying: A resource guide for parents and teachers, Campaign Against Bullying,*** Attic Press, 1995.

Neil Duncan: ***Sexual bullying: Gender conflict and pupil culture in secondary schools,*** Routledge, 1999.

Sandra Brown: ***Where there is evil,*** Macmillan, 1998.

Melita Schaum & Karen Parish; ***Salked: Breaking the Silence in America***, Simon & Schuster, 1995.

Jessica Kingsley: ***New Perspectives on Bullying.***

Ken Rigby: ***Bulling in Schools and What to do about it.***

Joseph Blase & Jo Blase: ***Breaking the silence: Overcoming the problem of principal mistreatment of teachers,*** Corwin Press, 2002.

WEB CONNECTIONS

Tim Field (Success Unlimited - public speaking) Bully OnLine (web page) The Field Foundation www.successunlimited.co.uk www.bullyonline.org www.thefieldfoundation.org

UK The Andrea Adams trust www.andreaadamstrust.org

Mental Health Network www.mhnet.org/guide/trauma.htm

The Healing Centre Online www.healing-arts.org

Prolonged Adaption Stress Syndrome
www.benzinger.org/pass.html

Canadian Traumatic Stress Network
www.Play.psych.mun.ca/~dhart/trauma_net/index.html

Australian Trauma Web www.psy.uq.edu.au/PTSD

PTSD sites www.ptsd.com

Sam Vaknin, (narcississm)

www.geocities.com/vaksam/index/htm

Anthony M. Benis (narcissism) www.Narcissm.homestead.com

Joanna Ashmun (narcissism) www.halcyon.com/jmashmun/npd

Lifeline www.lifelinemacarthur.org.au

Together we do better www.togetherwedobetter.vic.gov.au

Buddy Bear – The Alanah and Madeline Foundation

www.buddybear.com.au jepcaa@internex.net.au

SOFWeb eduweb.vic.gov.au/bullying/index.htm

Bullying Everybody's Business

www.kidshelp.com.au/info7/contents.htm

Reach Out! www.reachout.com.au

Mind Matters online.curriculum.edu.au mindmatters/index.htm

Judith Paphazy, Resilience Promotion jepcaa@internex.net.au

Peer Support Foundation Victoria psupport@peersupport.com.au
Stop Bullying! bevans@alphalink.com.au
West Education Centre: **Beat Bullying** wested@ozemail.com.au
Eliminating violence -Managing Anger www.ses.org.nz
No Bullying Starts Today luckyduck@dial.pipex.com
Police/Telecom "Stop Bullying" www.nobully.org.nz
Bullying Online (UK) www.bulying.co.uk
Scottish anti-bullying Network, Edinburgh abn@mhie.ac.uk
Anti-bully www.antibully.org.uk
UK Dept for Ed & Employment DfEE
    www.dfee.gov.uk/bullying/pages/home.html
The Wounded Child Project www.thewoundedchild.org
Selwyn College Anti-Harassment Team (New Zealand)
    www.aht-selwyn.school.nz
Dutch school bullying www.pesten.net
QIEU Bullying Policies www.qieu.asn.au
Bullying in USA www.bullypolice.org
Communities Against Violence Network www.cavnet.org
National Criminal Justice Reference Service www.ncjrs.org
Stalking Resource Center (SRC) www.ncvc.org/src/index.html
Anti-stalking web site www.antistalking.com
The Stalking Assistance Site www.stalkingassistance.com
Survivors of Stalking (SOS) www.soshelp.org
The Stalking Victims Sanctuary www.stalkingvictims.com
Victim Advocacy Program of the Capital District VACCD@aol.com
Victim-Assistance Online www.vaonline.org
Stalking FAQ www.state.ia.us/government/ag/stalker.htm
National Victim Centre www.ojp.usdoj.gov/ovc/help/stalk/info44.htm

Cyberstalking www.cyberangels.org/stalking

The Message Relay Center www.MessageRelayCenter.msn.com

Not Victims www.smalltime.com/notvictims

Harassment law UK www.harassment-law.co.uk

Beyond Bullying ww.cwpp.slp.pld.gov.au/bba/default.html

Beyond Bullying www.bulliesincorporated.co.nz

The Mobbing Encyclopaedia www.leymann.se/English/frame.html

National Union of Teachers www.teachers.org.uk

Northern Territory Work Health (2001) www.nt.gov.au/dib/wha

WorkCover Authority of New South Wales (2001)
    www.workcover.nsw.gov.au

WorkCover Corporation, South Australia (2001)
    www.workcover.com

Workplace Standards Tasmania (2001)

www.safetyline.wa.gov.au

New Perspectives on Bullying - Astam Books, Australia
    info@astambooks.com.au

UK National Work Stress Network www.workstress.net

Befrienders International (Suicide) wwwlbefrienders.org

Helene Richards and Sheila Freeman
    www.sheilafreemanconsulting.biz/bullying.htm

Canada safety Council
    www.safety-council.org/info/OSH/bullies.html

Australian Manufacturing Workers' Union www.amwu.asn.au

Symptoms of emotional abuse
    www.lilaclane.com/relationships/emotional-abuse

Beating bullies in New Zealand www.bulliesincorporated.co.nz

South Australian Employee Ombudsman Gary Collis
www.employeeombudsman.sa.gov.au
www.oeo.sa.gov.au

Working Women's Centre S.A. www.wwc.org.au

Women's Executive Network - Canada
www.wxnetwork.com

Citizens Against Bulling Association (CABA) of Northern Alberta Canada www.stopbullyingme.ab.ca caba@stopbullyingme.ab.ca

Dr. Arnold Nerenberg - Road rage www.roadrage.com

Workplace Services SA www.eric.sa.gov.au

Equal Opportunity SA www.eoc.sa.gov.au

Industrial Court SA www.industrialcourt.sa.gov.au

Acts and regulations SA
www.parliament.sa.gov.au/dbsearch/legsearch.htm

Spanish Website www.psicoter.es

The Canadian Safe School Network
www.cssn.org/pages/home.htm

The Workers Health Centre ACT www.workershealth.com.au admin@workershealth.com.au

ACTU *"Work on Life"* e-bulletin www.actu.asn.au

Australian Services Union - workplace bullying
asuclerical-nsw.asn.au/campaigns/w.html

International Labour Organisation, Geneva www.ilo.org

New Zealand Council of Trade Unions union.org.nz

UnionSafe, NSW unionsafe.labor.net.au

www.ingramcontent.com/pod-product-compliance
Lightning Source LLC
LaVergne TN
LVHW051550070426
835507LV00021B/2499